Academic Program Reviews:
Institutional Approaches, Expectations, and Controversies

by Clifton F. Conrad and Richard F. Wilson

ASHE-ERIC Higher Education Report No. 5, 1985

Prepared by

Clearinghouse on Higher Education –
The George Washington University

Published by

Association for the Study of Higher Education

Jonathan D. Fife,
Series Editor

Cite as
Conrad, Clifton F. and Wilson, Richard F. *Academic Program Reviews: Institutional Approaches, Expectations, and Controversies*. ASHE-ERIC Higher Education Report No. 5. Washington, D.C.: Association for the Study of Higher Education, 1985.

The ERIC Clearinghouse on Higher Education invites individuals to submit proposals for writing monographs for the Higher Education Report series. Proposals must include:
1. A detailed manuscript proposal of not more than five pages.
2. A 75-word summary to be used by several review committees for the initial screening and rating of each proposal.
3. A vita.
4. A writing sample.

Library of Congress Catalog Card Number 85-073508
ISSN 0884-0040
ISBN 0-913317-24-1

ERIC® **Clearinghouse on Higher Education**
The George Washington University
One Dupont Circle, Suite 630
Washington, D.C. 20036

ASHE **Association for the Study of Higher Education**
One Dupont Circle, Suite 630
Washington, D.C. 20036

This publication was partially prepared with funding from the National Institute of Education, U.S. Department of Education under contract no. 400-82-0011. The opinions expressed in this report do not necessarily reflect the positions or policies on NIE or the Department.

EXECUTIVE SUMMARY

Within the last few years, the role of academic program review has emerged as one of the most salient issues in American higher education. Nestled within a context of accountability, program reviews have become a dominant and controversial activity at the institutional, system, and state levels. Although statutory or constitutional authority varies greatly, higher education agencies in all 50 states now conduct state-level reviews; 28 of those agencies have authority to discontinue programs. Moreover, a majority of the multicampus systems have introduced program reviews, and over three-fourths of the nation's colleges and universities employ some type of program review (Barak 1982). The heightened interest in program review can be traced to a widespread interest in improving program quality and the need to respond creatively to severe financial constraints and to external constituencies' expectations for accountability.

The literature contains a generous amount of controversy regarding the purposes, processes, and outcomes of program review. The intent of this monograph is to illuminate this terrain: to capture the diverse institutional approaches to review, to examine the central issues, and to reflect on ways in which program review might be improved. Toward that end, the report is based on a review of the literature and an analysis of program review practices at 30 representative institutions.

What Distinguishes Current Program Reviews?

Colleges and universities have a long-standing tradition of program evaluation, a tradition that can be traced from colonial and antebellum colleges to modern American universities. The origins of program evaluation can be found in such developments as the elimination of Greek and Latin as entrance requirements and the introduction of mathematics, modern languages, and the social sciences. Until well into this century, program reviews were viewed largely as internal matters, initiated most often to reform and revitalize the curriculum. The idea that program reviews should be conducted to demonstrate accountability to external constituencies is a phenomenon of the twentieth century. The gradual development of regional and professional accrediting associations and the creation of statewide governing and coordinating boards are at least partly the result of a belief that programs must be responsive to the needs and expectations of external as well as internal audiences.

Especially in the last several years, program reviews have been designed to achieve another major objective: aiding those making decisions about the reallocation of resources and program discontinuance. Thus, a broad range of expectations now exists for program review in higher education. Program improvement, accountability to external constituencies, and resource reallocation are the purposes cited most often. Despite this growth in expectations, little evidence suggests that an evaluation system can be designed to address multiple purposes simultaneously. It is especially difficult to pursue both program improvement and resource reallocation at the same time (Barak 1982; George 1982), and an institution's interests are served best if reviews focused on program improvement are conducted separately from those concerned with reallocating resources.

What Do Formal Evaluation Models Contribute to Program Reviews in Higher Education?

Program reviews at most institutions draw heavily on one or more of several models: goal-based, responsive, decision-making, or connoisseurship. Although these models are seldom explicitly identified in descriptions of institutional review processes, they can be inferred from the procedures used.

The *goal-based model* has had the most influence, offering the advantages of systematic attention to how a program has performed in relation to what was intended and of a concern for the factors contributing to success or failure. The characteristic of the *responsive model* that has influenced program reviews in higher education is the attention given to program activities and effects, regardless of what its goals might be. The central concern of an evaluation, according to a proponent of responsive evaluation, ought to be the issues and concerns of those who have an interest in the program, not how a program has performed relative to its formal goal statements (Stake 1975).

The major contribution of the *decision-making model* to program review in higher education is the explicit attempt to link evaluations with decision making, thus focusing the evaluation and increasing the likelihood that results will be used. The *connoisseurship model* of evaluation has a long tradition in higher education. It relies heavily on the perspectives and judgments of experts, which are valued because of the individual's assumed superior knowledge and expertise and a commonly shared value system (Gardner 1977).

It is unlikely that an institution would want to develop an evaluation system that strictly conforms to any of these models. Their value lies in their varying perspectives on how evaluations should occur. The use of features from each model can enrich evaluations and is more likely to yield useful results.

How Should Quality Be Assessed?

The assessment of quality has generated more confusion and debate than any other issue for those engaged in program review. Pressure to define what quality means and what types of information should be collected has always existed, but interest has been heightened by the relatively recent emphasis on program review for resource reallocation and retrenchment.

Four different perspectives have been offered on how quality should be defined: the reputational view, the resources view, the outcomes view, and the value-added view. The *reputational view* assumes that quality cannot be measured directly and is best inferred through the judgments of experts in the field. The *resources view* emphasizes the human, financial, and physical assets available to a program. It assumes that high quality exists when resources like excellent students, productive and highly qualified faculty, and modern facilities and equipment are prevalent.

The *outcomes view* of quality draws attention from resources to the quality of the product. Faculty publications, students' accomplishments following graduation, and employers' satisfaction with program graduates, for example, are indicators used. The problem with the outcomes view is that the program's contribution to the success of graduates, for example, is not isolated. It is assumed that if the graduate is a success, the program is a success.

The *value-added view* directs attention to what the institution has contributed to a student's education (Astin

1980). The focus of the value-added view is on what a student has learned while enrolled. In turn, programs are judged on how much they add to a student's knowledge and personal development. The difficulty with this view of quality is how to isolate that contribution.

Most institutions assess quality by adopting aspects of all four views. The assumption is that quality has multiple dimensions and, in turn, that multiple indicators should be used for its assessment. A large number of quantitative and qualitative indicators have been suggested for making such assessments (Clark, Hartnett, and Baird 1976; Conrad and Blackburn 1985). The specific indicators to be used and the weight to be assigned to each should vary by institution. Such an approach recognizes the difficulty of making qualitative judgments and suggests that they will be more accurate if different dimensions are measured and different perspectives solicited.

Do Program Reviews Make a Difference?
Perhaps the most significant issue relating to program review is the effect of the considerable activity at all levels of higher education. The assessment of impact requires that attention be given to the longer-term effects of decisions that are made, that is, whether a program is stronger, more efficient, or of higher quality. The major criterion to use in assessing impact is whether an evaluation makes a system function better (Cronbach 1977). In conducting such assessments, evaluators must pay attention to effects that are latent as well as manifest, incremental as well as radical, subtle as well as obvious.

Only a few studies have analyzed impact systematically. The University of California (Smith 1979) and the University of Iowa (Barak 1982) benefited from program reviews, including providing a stimulus for change and improving knowledge among decision makers about programs. Not all analyses of impact are as positive, however. A small number of studies (Skubal 1979; Smith 1979) have focused on cost savings and have found that little money is saved—that, in fact, reviews frequently require an increased commitment. Program reviews can have negative effects—unwarranted anxiety, diversion of time from teaching and research, and unfulfilled promises and expectations (Seeley 1981).

The continued existence and growth of program review processes suggest that such efforts are supported and that the results can be beneficial. Some believe that reviews do not make much difference, however, and may actually make things worse. The studies of impact provide insufficient evidence for deciding which view is more correct. Given the plethora of program reviews at all levels of higher education, the need to study the effects of such reviews more systematically is urgent.

ADVISORY BOARD

Roger Baldwin
Assistant Professor of Education
College of William and Mary

Robert Birnbaum
Professor of Higher Education
Teachers College, Columbia University

Susan W. Cameron
Assistant Professor and Chair
Higher/Postsecondary Education
Syracuse University

Clifton F. Conrad
Professor of Higher Education
University of Arizona

George D. Kuh
Associate Dean for Academic Affairs
School of Education
Indian University

Yvonna S. Lincoln
Associate Professor of Higher Education
The University of Kansas

Robert A. Scott
President
Ramapo College of New Jersey

CONSULTING EDITORS

Robert Atwell
President
American Council on Education

Robert Barak
Deputy Executive Secretary
Director of Academic Affairs and Research
Iowa State Board of Regents

Larry Braskamp
Assistant to the Vice Chancellor
    for Academic Affairs
University of Illinois

Robert Cope
Professor of Higher Education
University of Washington

Robert L. Craig
Former Vice President, Government Affairs
American Society for Training and Development, Inc.

John W. Creswell
Associate Professor
Department of Educational Administration
University of Nebraska

Mary F. Fox
Associate Professor
Center for Research on Social Organization
University of Michigan

W. Lee Hansen
Professor
Department of Economics
University of Wisconsin

David Kaser
Professor
School of Library and Information Science
Indiana University

George Keller
Senior Vice President
Barton-Gillet Company

David W. Leslie
Professor and Chair
Department of Educational Leadership
The Florida State University

Ernest A. Lynton
Commonwealth Professor and Senior Associate
Center for the Study of Policy and the Public Interest
University of Massachusetts

Gerald W. McLaughlin
Institutional Research and Planning Analysis
Virginia Polytechnic Institute and State University

Theodore J. Marchese
Vice President
American Association for Higher Education

L. Jackson Newell
Professor and Dean
University of Utah

Harold Orlans
Office of Programs and Policy
United States Civil Rights Commission

Lois S. Peters
Center for Science and Technology Policy
New York University

John M. Peterson
Director, Technology Planning
The B. F. Goodrich Company

Richard H. Quay
Social Science Librarian
Miami University

John E. Stecklein
Professor of Educational Psychology
University of Minnesota

James H. Werntz, Jr.
Vice Chancellor for Academic Affairs
University of North Carolina

CONTENTS

FOREWORD

Although academic program reviews have been conducted in one form or another for more than 50 years, only in the last 15 have they become a major method for change or reorientation in the academic community. The review process is a complicated one, however, that needs to be examined carefully.

Before academic program review is undertaken potential sources of problems should be identified and eliminated as much as possible. Three distinct aspects of program review can harbor problems: the stated purpose, anticipated outcomes, and the conflict between the two. A vaguely defined purpose (e.g., "programs must be reviewed regularly") is of little use to those conducting a review. The purpose of a review should be concise and clearly enunciated. Anticipated outcomes also must be clearly stated since they may not be obtainable via the chosen method of review. Problems will arise if the purpose and anticipated outcomes are contradictory or if too much is asked of a single review. It should be acknowledged, for example, that a single academic program review cannot at the same time improve quality and make program discontinuance decisions. The question to be asked is: What is the use of the review and how are the results to be applied? To be effective, a program review must be understood in terms of precise purposes, clear outcomes, and alternative review methods.

Where does the impetus initially come from to review a particular program? Generally, faculty members have enough influence through department meetings, curriculum selection, and faculty gatherings to shape their own programs without resorting to a formal review process. Therefore the impetus for program review usually comes from an external source. Five distinct bodies may initiate the action leading to a program review: students within a program, non-program faculty, administrators, accrediting bodies, and state-level agencies. It is helpful to understand each group's focus or motive before charging the investigative committee. For example, students within a program will complain if it does not meet their expectations. They may be concerned with the student-teacher ratio, the number of teaching assistants, or the connection between coursework and getting a job. Other faculty members may request a program review if they suspect a disproportionate workload or perceive that a particular program adversely affects the institution's overall academic reputation.

Administrators, faced with shrinking resources, may call for a cost-effectiveness review. Accrediting bodies are usually concerned with a consistent minimum standard of quality for similar programs. Finally, state-level agencies call for program reviews to insure that different institutions do not compete within a similar geographic area. It is clear that by identifying the primary purpose of a review and delineating the needed outcome, institutions can conduct academic program reviews with maximum efficiency.

It is important to establish priorities and determine the primary purpose for a particular review. A quality control review aims to assess, maintain, and improve program quality. The goal may be open-ended and make any recommendations that will improve the program. If cost-effectiveness is the purpose, then the outcome may be to recommend ways to cut back current costs while minimizing the impact on program quality. Likewise, if the purpose of the review is to eliminate duplication of efforts within a single system, then the desired outcome may be program discontinuance. Different purposes will produce different outcomes, just as different groups will have different aims in requesting a program review. Determining the purpose will help choose the proper review model and outcomes.

There is a need to better understand the purpose behind academic program review, different methods of program review, possible outcomes, and implementation of the results. The authors, Clifton Conrad, professor of higher education at the University of Arizona, and Richard Wilson, assistant vice-chancellor for academic affairs at the University of Illinois, address these issues by examining different approaches to academic program review. Since the choice of a model has a major impact on the results obtained, a clear understanding of the intended purpose and outcomes is needed before selecting the evaluative tool to use. The methods of program evaluation differ not only in the type and number of persons required, but also in the method of data collection.

This ASHE-ERIC report, the fifth in the 1985 series, does a particularly fine job in giving concrete examples of institutional practices. It also shows that one area of concern should be the impact of a review on the faculty. Perhaps the most difficult part of academic program reviews is implementing the recommendations once they have been made. Clearly stated purposes and outcomes help prepare various groups for positive changes after the report has been completed. Future areas of study might include the value of conducting follow-up studies to determine if the recommendations were implemented, the extent to which they were successful, and whether the purposes and outcomes of the review were actually achieved. Academic program reviews are and will continue to be a major tool in all levels of institutional management.

Jonathan D. Fife
Series Editor
Professor and Director
ERIC Clearinghouse on Higher Education
The George Washington University

PROGRAM REVIEW IN PERSPECTIVE

Within the last decade, the role of academic program review has emerged as one of the most prominent issues in American higher education. Many faculty, staff, administrators, governing boards, and state higher education agencies have become deeply—sometimes passionately—involved in program review. To place recent developments in perspective, this introduction considers the antecedents of current review efforts, as found in a long-standing tradition of program evaluation in American higher education, and discusses the growth of three major types of academic program review in the last 15 years.

"Program evaluation" refers to a range of activities concerned broadly with the assessment of new or existing programs. "Program review" is a subset of program evaluation and refers exclusively to the evaluation of existing programs.

Historical Antecedents

The contemporary concern with program review is rooted in a tradition of program evaluation that finds its origin in the seventeenth century, with the development of Harvard College. Program evaluation at the nation's first college took place as early as 1642, when the first nine graduates of Harvard were given a public final examination by the external Board of Overseers. On the day of the first commencement in America, students were required to demonstrate their learning in the classical languages and their skills in disputation on both philological and philosophical theses. The first Harvard degrees were conferred on those students who "received the approbation of the overseers" owing to "their proficiency in the tongues of the arts" (Morrison 1935, pp. 256–59). The tradition of academic program evaluation that began at Harvard has, in various forms, continued to the present.

From the seventeenth century until well into the nineteenth century, control of the academic program—even down to the selection of textbooks—rested mostly in the hands of institutional lay boards. Program evaluation was infrequent and, in most colleges, aimed primarily at improving the overall academic program, such as the elimination of Greek and Latin as entrance requirements and the introduction of natural philosophy (science), mathematics, and modern languages (Conrad and Wyer 1980, p. 10).

Most institutions held firmly to the classical curriculum, and major changes in educational programs were considered unnecessary, even heretical (Harcleroad 1980, p. 4).

Despite the influence of the Yale Report of 1828, which defended the classical curriculum and proved a temporary barrier against democratic forces pressing for control of higher education and fundamental academic reform (Conrad 1978), demands for change in the academic program increased as the century unfolded. Though usually infrequent, institutional reviews of academic program offerings marked a growing interest in program evaluation as a vehicle for revitalization. Disenchantment with the rigid classical curriculum of the antebellum college gradually led many colleges to evaluate the classical curriculum and, in some cases, to introduce reforms and innovations (Burke 1982).

Not until after the Civil War, however, did upheaval occur in the academic programs of most institutions. Many colleges and universities began to embrace the German ideal of research and the American ideal of service. As a result, graduate and professional education was introduced at many institutions, and the classical curriculum began to crumble as the establishment of the elective system provided a vehicle for introducing modern subjects like history, English, and economics. These widespread changes seemed to symbolize an increasingly self-conscious view among faculty and administrators of the importance of evaluating both existing and proposed programs. Furthermore, those changes reflected the influence of the strong administrative leadership of such university presidents as Andrew White at Cornell and Charles Eliot at Harvard. No less telling was the emergence of the professoriate as an important voice in academic decision making. As faculty grew in size and professional stature, as more specialized subjects were incorporated into the curriculum, and as institutions grew in size and complexity, control of decisions about academic programs moved increasingly away from institutional governing boards and toward administrative and faculty control (Harcleroad 1980, p. 9).

The pattern of academic program evaluation established in the latter part of the 1800s continued well into the twentieth century. At most institutions, programs were occasionally evaluated, usually informally as administrative leadership and concerned faculty joined to evaluate existing programs and to consider changes in the formal course of study. An illustration of this pattern can be found in developments that transpired at Harvard in 1909. President A. Lawrence Lowell, with the support of the faculty, introduced a program in general education designed to curb excessive elective freedom, overspecialization, and the perceived lack of educational unity in the undergraduate curriculum (Conrad and Wyer 1980, p. 15).

The twentieth century has witnessed the gradual development of external forms of academic program evaluation, notably accreditation by professional organizations and program reviews by statewide boards of higher education. Professional and regional accreditation, both voluntary and aimed at promoting minimum standards of quality, developed into major evaluative forces during the twentieth century. The first of six regional accreditation bodies was established in 1885, and specialized accreditation in such fields as medicine and law took root during the first few decades of the new century. Especially after 1950, most institutions accepted voluntary accreditation: In the subsequent two decades, regional associations and as many as 27 specialized associations accredited over 2,600 institutions (Orlans 1975, pp. 16–23).

Although six states had established a statewide governing board for public higher education by 1900, the emergence of such boards is primarily a phenomenon of the twentieth century. While only voluntary forms of institutional cooperation existed in many states during the first half of the current century, other states began to establish state higher education agencies: Ten states created statewide governing boards, and two created statewide coordinating agencies (Harcleroad 1980, pp. 8–9). All of these state agencies were given some type of responsibility for academic program review and approval in addition to budget approval (Millard 1976).

While the term "academic program review" was not used at the time, some state boards with responsibilities for program review exercised that power. Several of the statewide boards "moved aggressively to reduce program duplication; in Georgia, the agency founded in the Depression year of 1931 eliminated ten institutions" (Berdahl 1971, p. 27).

To encourage the wise use of limited funds to meet state

Many colleges and universities began to embrace the German ideal of research and the American ideal of service.

educational needs, the major expansion of statewide governing and coordinating boards took place between 1950 and 1970. By 1969, 19 states had statewide governing boards, 27 had coordinating boards, only one had a voluntary form of interinstitutional cooperation, and three had no formal coordination (Harcleroad 1980, p. 10). Like those boards established before 1950, most of the newly established state agencies gradually developed formal program review procedures to assess proposed new programs and to evaluate existing programs. Because program evaluation became standard practice in many states during the growth of the late 1950s and 1960s, evaluating new programs rather than established ones was emphasized heavily.

By the end of the 1960s, various types of program evaluation had a long history in American higher education. On one level, internal program review by faculty and administrators occurred in response to pressures for changed and improved programs. On another level, external program evaluations by accrediting agencies and statewide higher education agencies were designed to satisfy the accountability requirements of various constituencies. Especially with the growth and influence of external program evaluation in the 1950s and 1960s, it became clear that state and institutional program evaluation had become an increasingly formal, systematic process. While the foundation for program evaluation had been laid, however, it was not until the 1970s that forces largely outside the academy were to make program review (internal as well as external) a central feature of academic program planning in the majority of institutions and states.

Growth of Program Review
The growth of program review over the last 15 years has derived from complex, interacting societal and educational forces. Several factors have contributed to the expanded use of program review:

- widespread interest in maintaining and improving the quality of higher learning, both from within and without the academy, in a period of diminishing resources available to higher education;
- new academic management techniques, such as stra-

tegic approaches to academic program planning and
budgeting (Barak 1981, p. 214);
● severe financial strains on higher education caused by
declining enrollments, inflation and recession,
increased costs, and overall shrinking financial support (Dougherty 1981);
● external demands for institutional and programmatic
accountability from taxpayers, legislators, student
consumers, and other constituencies;
● demands from governing boards and campus administrators for more effective and efficient use of limited
resources.

Within the context of retrenchment and accountability
and a rising tide of concern about institutional and program
quality, program reviews have assumed a heightened sense
of importance at both state and institutional levels. Not
surprisingly, since the early 1970s they have been oriented
increasingly toward program accountability as much as
program improvement: Existing programs have been given
greater scrutiny with an eye toward the reallocation of
resources, reorganization, and program discontinuance.
   In addition to the continuing presence of accreditation as
a major vehicle for program evaluation, three major types
of program review have been dominant in higher education
over the past 15 years: reviews by state higher education
agencies, multicampus system reviews, and institutional
reviews.

State-level reviews
During the last 15 years, the states' involvement in academic program review has expanded markedly, both by
approving proposed new programs and by reviewing existing programs (Barak and Berdahl 1978; Green 1981). While
a few states, such as Wisconsin and Virginia, introduced
legislative and executive audits or reviews during the 1970s
(Berdahl 1977), most of the growth in state-level review
has taken place among higher education agencies.[1] In general, responsibilities for approval of state-level programs
have coincided with the growth of state agencies themselves: As agencies have acquired broad discretionary
powers, their responsibilities for approving programs have
also grown. In the last decade alone, a number of agencies

that previously had authority only to recommend have been given increased regulatory responsibility. Many agencies that formerly had weak responsibility for approving programs now have greater authority because of expanded budgetary responsibilities (Barak 1982, p. 27). In most states, the final authority on new programs has shifted from institutions to state-level higher education agencies.

By 1981, statewide agencies or governing boards in 43 states were involved in at least some new program approval for public institutions: 33 had authority to approve programs in the public sector, and 10 could review programs and make recommendations. Of these 43 states, nine also conducted new program approval for independent institutions; five agencies had authority to actually approve programs in the independent sector, while four could conduct reviews and make recommendations (Barak 1982, p. 27). While the statutory powers, organizational structures, scope of authority, and approaches to evaluation vary considerably across state higher education agencies, nearly all of these agencies now are responsible for approving new programs.

It comes as no surprise, in an era of retrenchment and accountability, that state higher education agencies also have been increasingly active in reviewing existing programs, a responsibility that previously was reserved almost exclusively for the academic community (Folger 1977, p. viii). Within the last decade, highly publicized state-level reviews have taken place in New York, Washington, Florida, and Louisiana (Barak 1977; Bogue 1980; Feasley 1980; Russo, Brown, and Rothweiler 1977).

The states' involvement in program review is growing (Barak and Berdahl 1978; Barak and Engdahl 1980; Berve 1975; Wilson and Miller 1980). In 1970, only a handful of statewide higher education agencies conducted program reviews. Today, all 50 states have some sort of reviewing process, although the statutory or constitutional authority of state agencies varies greatly, ranging from no authority to limited authority for reviewing certain programs at certain levels (graduate or undergraduate) to broad authority to review all programs for institutions at all levels. Moreover, some agencies represent only the public sector or a segment of the public sector, while a few others have authority in the independent sector as well. A recent survey found that 28 state higher education agencies have the authority to discontinue at least some programs, even though this authority sometimes is limited to just one institutional segment (Barak 1982, p. 54). Not surprisingly, a few state agencies exercise authority beyond their statutory or constitutional authority; others exercise less.

In addition to differences in their authority over program review, organizational structure and methods of evaluation differ across the states. State agencies have taken two major approaches to evaluation. Roughly a dozen state-level agencies share responsibilities for review with colleges and universities. In these states—Illinois and California, for example—responsibility for review rests largely with individual institutions, though agencies in these states also may conduct reviews across all institutions in a particular discipline or cluster of disciplines. In the majority of states, however, state agencies assume the major responsibility for reviewing the programs of public institutions, relying on a combination of outside consultants and agency staff (Barak 1981, p. 216; Barak 1982, pp. 55–60). While state agencies display diversity in levels of authority over and methods of program evaluation, nearly all states now engage in some form of approval of new programs and review of existing programs.

Multicampus system reviews
Nearly all program review activity in multicampus systems has developed in the last 15 years. Early in the 1970s, systemwide reviews—either of proposed or of existing programs—seldom were conducted (Lee and Bowen 1971). By the middle of the decade, however, multicampus reviews of proposed new programs were common, and existing graduate and professional programs were reviewed periodically in seven of nine multicampus systems studied in one survey (Lee and Bowen 1975). In each of the 19 multicampus systems of higher education in the country in 1975, the governing board and its staff had at least some authority to evaluate new programs proposed by system institutions and/or to eliminate or otherwise to change existing programs (Barak and Berdahl 1978).

Today, nearly all multicampus systems conduct some kind of program approval. Many systems are attempting to upgrade the effectiveness of their evaluations of proposed new programs by such measures as using outside consultants (Barak 1982, pp. 25–27). Moreover, at least half of the multicampus systems for both four-year institutions and community colleges now undertake some level of review of existing programs (Barak 1982, p. 49). Studies in this area, however, have not found a relationship between program review and the size of the multicampus system. Nor does the presence or absence of program reviews by a state board seem to relate to the degree of review in multicampus systems. In some states, both the coordinating board and the system office review programs, while in other states, the system office does not conduct separate reviews (Barak 1982, p. 51).

Some states show considerable overlap in the legal authority over program review between the governing boards of multicampus systems and state-level coordinating boards (Smith 1980, p. 43). While some multicampus systems do not conduct program reviews or else limit their reviews simply to monitoring state-level or institutional reviews, some have introduced more comprehensive system-level reviews in the last few years. In California, for example, system-level reviews have become second in importance only to institutional reviews; the state coordinating board (the California Commission on Postsecondary Education) limits its role to monitoring system-level reviews. In short, program reviews by multicampus systems have become increasingly visible in recent years.

Institutional reviews

Most postsecondary institutions always have had procedures for approving new programs, but the procedures usually were informal, and a new program of study often could be introduced with little difficulty. During the last 15 years, however, program approval procedures have become much more formal. Nearly all postsecondary institutions now have a program-approval process, though final approval for new programs in all but seven states rests in the state higher education agency. In recent years, however, the major expansion of academic program evaluation by institutions has been in terms of the formal review of existing programs (Munitz and Wright 1980, p. 21). While concern about quality clearly has provided an impetus to internal program review, the main reasons for this growth derive from institutional concerns over the effective use of scarce resources and from greater requirements for accountability from external constituencies, especially state-level higher education agencies (Wilson 1984, p. 143).

In the mid-1970s, a publication of the Carnegie Council on Policy Studies in Higher Education predicted that institutions would come to rely much more heavily on program and course evaluation (Glenny et al. 1976). This prediction has proven accurate. In a survey for the National Center for Higher Education Management Systems, a study that used a stratified sample of approximately one-third of the nation's postsecondary institutions, 82 percent of the institutions surveyed reported that they employed some type of formal program review (Barak 1982, pp. 34–35). (All of the survey respondents did not respond to the same definition of "program review"; a few institutions identified annual budget reviews and even regional accreditation reviews as program reviews.) In addition, 2 percent of the sample reported the use of an informal process of program review. Only about 16 percent of the responding institutions indicated that they did not conduct program reviews.

The study also found that the majority of institutions initiated their present program review policies after 1970, and more than half said their reviews were developed after 1975. Although large research universities were more likely than community colleges, small independent colleges, proprietary schools, and predominantly black institutions to engage in internal program review, the predominant trend is for institutions to engage in some formal evaluation of existing programs.

In summary, program review in higher education has surged within the last 15 years. Rooted in a long-standing tradition of institutional attention to program quality and shaped on the anvil of a period of retrenchment and accountability, academic program review has emerged as a central area of concern in higher education. Consonant with the external pressures acting upon higher education, much of the impetus for program review has come from the states in the form of legislative reviews or audits and reviews by state-level coordinating boards. Multicampus system reviews and institutional reviews, however, have emerged of late as perhaps less visible but no less dominating a feature of higher education. Notwithstanding the

82 percent of the institutions surveyed reported that they employed some type of formal program review.

inevitable concern and controversy surrounding its emergence, academic program review in American higher education has come of age.

Focus

The remainder of this monograph focuses on campus-based, or institutional, academic program reviews. In light of the importance now placed on the review of existing academic programs at the institutional level, this inquiry centers exclusively on such reviews. The definition of program review used in this monograph is adopted from Craven (1980b, p. 434): *Academic program review refers to the process of defining, collecting, and analyzing information about an existing program or noninstructional unit to arrive at a judgment about the continuation, modification, enhancement, or termination of the program or unit.*

1. "Higher education agencies" is used to refer to the agency (or board) responsible for coordinating public higher education in a state. These agencies, which are sometimes called "state coordinating boards," have varying responsibilities, most often in the areas of planning, budgeting, and program review. In most states, the state agency exists at a level above institutional boards or system boards. In states where all public higher education is in one system, the system board, by definition, is the statewide higher education agency.

DIVERSE APPROACHES TO PROGRAM REVIEW

Launched on the turbulent seas of the last decade in response to a variety of pressures, institutional reviews of existing programs have left in their wakes no single preferred way to design and implement program reviews. This chapter sketches the diverse approaches by examining six major dimensions cutting across all program review efforts: the purposes of program review, the selection of programs for review, program reviewers, models for evaluation, evaluative criteria, and methodological approaches. Alternative approaches and practices are identified and discussed for each dimension.

Purposes

Until the last few years, the single overriding reason for conducting program reviews at most institutions was to improve academic programs. In the late 1970s, for example, a report by the Committee on Internal Program Review of the Council of Graduate Schools stated unequivocally that "the purpose of a well-conducted review process is to help the program improve" (Gentile 1980, p. 7). At about the same time, a national survey of institutions found that the most commonly cited reason for conducting institutional program reviews was to improve programs (Barak 1982, p. 39).

The literature abounds with case studies of institutions in which assessment for improvement serves as the driving purpose behind program review. For example, program improvement is the major purpose of program review at Ohio State University, the University of Nebraska–Lincoln, the University of Illinois, the University of Iowa, and the Metropolitan Community College District in Kansas City, Missouri (Arns and Poland 1980; Barak 1982; DiBiaso and Ecker 1982; Seagren and Bean 1981; Wilson 1984).

In addition to improving programs, other compelling reasons for conducting program reviews have surfaced in recent years: to meet state-level mandates for reviews; to demonstrate institutional responsiveness to constituencies, such as sponsoring denominations or community groups; to provide a foundation for allocating and reallocating resources; to provide information to decision makers considering program discontinuance; and, in the case of two-year institutions, to respond to federal requirements for the evaluation of occupational programs. Usually, several of

these reasons provide the impetus for initiating program reviews at an institution. For many institutions, adding an additional statement of purpose has been a relatively painless way to build consensus for program review (Wilson 1984, p. 144). As a result, institutions display diversity in terms of the various constellations of purposes that inform their program review efforts.

Notwithstanding this diversity, the major differences across institutional program reviews pertain to their primary purposes. On the one hand, many institutions emphasize program improvement as the major purpose of program review. On the other hand, a growing number of institutions have embraced the reallocation of resources (including, in some cases, program reduction) as the driving force behind program review. And a large number of institutions have embraced both program improvement and resource reallocation as the two driving purposes in conducting program reviews.

Given the context of retrenchment and accountability confronting many postsecondary institutions, it is hardly surprising that the central purpose of program review in many institutions is driven by a desire to allocate and reallocate resources on a differential rather than an across-the-board basis. Next to program improvement, in one study, resource reallocation was the most frequently cited reason for conducting program reviews (Barak 1982, p. 39). Such institutions as the University of Vermont, Michigan State University, the University of Houston, and the University of Minnesota have connected program reviews to resource allocation (Arns and Poland 1980; Clugston 1984; Munitz and Wright 1980).

Perhaps the most telling feature of recent program reviews is that many institutions now view program review as a major vehicle for allocating and reallocating resources, thereby accomplishing more with existing resources. At the University of Louisville, for example, program reviews are examined by all of the vice presidents as well as by a planning staff that includes representatives from the planning office, budget office, and institutional research office. Thus, program review is linked closely with planning and budgeting, as indicated in two of the university's major objectives for program review:

1. To provide a basis for recommendations regarding
   a. internal allocations in the preparation of annual
      operating budgets and
   b. reallocations (in the form of budget adjustments)
      during the operating year and
2. To serve as a building block in an evolving planning
   process that will make planning and resource alloca-
   tion increasingly rational processes (Barak 1982, p.
   38).

Some institutions faced with declining resources have
gone so far as to use "program discontinuance"—including merging programs, eliminating curricula within departments, and closing entire departments, colleges, or noninstructional units—as a tool for reducing and reallocating
resources. For those institutions, a major purpose of program review is to provide a foundation for reducing the
scope of institutional program offerings so as to "extract
programs not meeting [program priorities] . . . to preserve
the vitality of those at the heart of the intellectual enter-
prise" (Shirley and Volkwein 1978, p. 486). The resources
saved are reallocated to existing programs or used to support new programs.

No exact figures are available regarding the number of
institutions that have made program discontinuance a
major consideration in program review, but more and more
institutions are moving in that direction. In response to
state-level mandates or declining resources, several public
institutions in the early to mid-1970s (the State University
of New York at Albany, for example) undertook reviews
that led to one or more programs' being discontinued. Others whose reviews during the last decade have led to programs' being cut include the University of California–
Berkeley, the University of California–Riverside, the University of Pennsylvania, Florida State University, the University of Wisconsin–Eau Claire, and the University of
Michigan (Dougherty 1979, 1981).

While most institutions involved in program review seem
to emphasize either program improvement or resource
reallocation (including program discontinuance), this examination of institutional reviews suggests that a substantial
number of institutions now combine both emphases as the

two driving purposes guiding program reviews. For example, until it recently placed a moratorium on program reviews, the University of Michigan conducted reviews aimed both at improving programs and reallocating resources, with the latter including program reduction (Dougherty 1981; Munitz and Wright 1980). Similarly, program review at the University of Tennessee at Knoxville emphasizes primarily these two purposes, as indicated in the institutional statement of review purposes:

- *To improve the quality of the University's academic offerings.*
- *To achieve the best use of resources.*
- *To foster cooperation among the academic and administrative units.*
- *To evaluate quality, productivity, need, and demand within the university, state, and region.*
- *To determine effectiveness and consider possible modifications.*
- *To facilitate academic planning and budgeting* (Office of the Provost 1984).

Program Selection
Although it has been addressed infrequently in the literature, the selection of programs to review is a critical decision. Colleges and universities involved in program review show diversity both in regard to whether programs are reviewed regularly or on an ad hoc basis and in terms of the particular mechanisms used to select programs for review.

Multicampus systems or state-level agencies now require public institutions in many states to review periodically all academic programs (graduate or undergraduate) and, in some cases, noninstructional units as well. Along with independent colleges and universities, these institutions have established a cycle of reviews in which all programs are reviewed regularly. At the State University of New York at Albany, for example, all departments are reviewed on a seven-year cycle (Dougherty 1979); Florida State University reviews all graduate programs on a five-year cycle.

In sharp contrast, some institutions conduct no regular reviews of academic programs but target programs for review on an ad hoc basis according to perceived need. Of

11 public universities that had conducted program reviews, four selected programs on an ad hoc or noncyclical basis (Dougherty 1979).

A few institutions combine regular reviews with in-depth, ad hoc reviews. For example, the University of Illinois at Urbana/Champaign has a two-stage program review process in which all units are reviewed periodically as part of the first stage of review. If problems are identified, a second stage, or in-depth, ad hoc review is conducted (Wilson 1984, p. 150). Thus, this two-stage process combines a regular review cycle with an additional ad hoc review where serious problems exist.

To avoid superficiality, most institutions involved in program review select only a limited number of programs for intensive review at any single time. This pattern holds true whether institutions rely on periodic or ad hoc reviews (or a combination of the two), although institutions with a regular cycle of reviews conduct many more reviews than do institutions employing ad hoc reviews only. Four major mechanisms are used to identify programs for intensive review: (1) logical clusters of programs or explicit criteria; (2) quantitative indicators; (3) the appointment of a new dean or department chair; and (4) as issues arise.

Institutions that review programs regularly normally select programs according to logical groupings (for example, all programs in the social sciences) or on the basis of a priori criteria. An example of the former is the University of California–Berkeley, which reviews six to eight graduate programs each year on the basis of logical clusters (Dougherty 1979). An example of the latter is the University of Nebraska–Lincoln, where 20 percent of all programs are selected for review each year on the basis of the following criteria:

> *Relationship of the program to other programs under review; marked change in student demand; planned program changes; accreditation cycles; and, elapsed time since last major budget review of budget, staffing, or program for any purpose* (Seagren and Bean 1981, p. 9).

For institutions conducting ad hoc reviews, some flagging mechanism is needed to trigger the selection of programs for review. The most typical approach is to use

Although it has been addressed infrequently in the literature, the selection of programs to review is a critical decision.

quantitative indicators such as cost effectiveness, degree productivity, student credit hours generated, faculty work loads, and various indicators of program quality. (Some institutions relying on the cyclical pattern employ quantitative indicators to begin their cycles.) In most institutions, only negative indicators trigger the review mechanism. A few institutions select one or two programs of high quality to review along with programs suspected of being relatively low in quality or having other negative indicators (Dougherty 1979). Institutions using quantitative indicators include the University of Wisconsin–Madison and the University of Wisconsin–Eau Claire (Dougherty 1979).

Although it is not a common practice, a few institutions review programs in conjunction with the appointment of a new dean or department chair. The rationale for this approach is that it provides valuable background information to the search committee and to the new appointee. A new chair or department head will know where to devote initial attention if a program review has been completed. Institutions using this approach include the University of Michigan and the University of Pennsylvania.

A growing number of institutions select programs for review as issues arise, such as when enrollment drops for a program, when a program receives a negative accreditation report, or when concerns are raised about the quality of the program. At the University of California–Berkeley, for example, the School of Criminology was reviewed because questions were raised about the quality of the program. Following a review of the school, which focused solely on qualitative considerations, the program was discontinued (Dougherty 1979). At the University of Michigan, the withdrawal of outside funds from the Population Planning Program, coupled with the request of the department for increased support, led to a review that resulted in the program's discontinuance.

In many colleges and universities, concerns about program quality and student demand have made certain fields especially vulnerable to ad hoc reviews. Education, for example, has become a popular target on many campuses, including the University of Kansas and the University of Arizona. Similarly, social work, library science, and humanities disciplines are being reviewed more frequently than other programs.

Program Reviewers

A critical dimension in any review process is the selection of evaluators to conduct the reviews. The process of selection is affected by the purposes of the review and the institutional style of governance. In many institutions, the responsibilities for review are assigned by a central review group or major administrator, often in consultation with a faculty senate and individuals representing the program under review. In other institutions, the central review group or administrator overseeing the review sets forth broad guidelines regarding the type(s) of reviewers to be used (for example, external evaluators), leaving the choice of evaluators to the program under review. In a few institutions, reviewers are selected jointly by a central review committee or administrator (or administrative group) and the program under review (Mims 1978).

Regardless of who selects the program reviewers, virtually all program reviews in higher education are established on the premise that program evaluation should be based on professional judgment. Notwithstanding this common feature, however, three general approaches to evaluation affect the selection of program reviewers: internal review, external review, and several combinations of internal and external review. Table 1 displays these alternative approaches.

Self-review or internal review probably is the dominant approach to evaluation in higher education. The tradition of internal self-evaluation is founded on the belief that program faculty best know the strengths and limitations of the program, and many institutions continue to make self-review the cornerstone of program review. Especially when the major purpose of program review is to improve the program, colleges and universities operate on the assumption that departmental or program faculty and in some instances students should be the primary reviewers. In the last few years, however, alternative and supplementary approaches to program review have become prevalent. Many institutions have chosen to give a much larger role to external program reviewers, that is, individuals not associated with the program under review.

External program review has begun to play a prominent role throughout higher education for a number of reasons. In many public colleges and universities, mandates for

TABLE 1
THREE APPROACHES TO SELECTING
PROGRAM REVIEWERS

Internal or Self-Review (internal reviewers)
- Program faculty
- Students in program (current and/or former)

External Review (external reviewers)
Within Institution
- Faculty peers (outside discipline or field being evaluated)
- Professional staff
Outside Institution
- Faculty peers (usually in discipline or field being evaluated)
- Professional evaluators

Internal/External Review (internal/external reviewers)
- Mixed review group
- Multiple reviews

Source: Adapted from Mims 1978, p. 11.

state-level and multicampus review require that external reviewers be an integral part of the process. No less telling, the context in which reviews are taking place has changed dramatically in the last few years in public and independent institutions alike. The principal purpose of program review has shifted increasingly away from program improvement to the reallocation of resources and even program discontinuance. As a result, many colleges and universities have turned to external reviews to enhance the objectivity and credibility of a review process that is intended to provide a foundation for making difficult decisions about the future of programs.

In an external review, program reviewers may be chosen from within the institution but external to the program under review or from outside the institution. In the former case, reviewers are usually faculty peers from outside the discipline or professional field being evaluated, though administrators and even students may also be involved. In a few institutions, professional staff who are experts on program evaluation participate in the review, but in most cases these individuals serve only as advisors (Wood and Davis 1978).

An increasingly common approach to external program

review is to employ review consultants from outside the college or university. In a small number of institutions, outside consultants with general backgrounds in program evaluation are hired to conduct the review. In most instances, however, professional evaluators are employed only to assist in designing the review process itself rather than to review programs. The more typical approach, which can be quite expensive, is to choose several faculty peers from other institutions who are in the same discipline or field as the program under review. One study of program review practices found that roughly half the institutions conducting reviews used faculty from other institutions as program reviewers (Barak 1982, p. 40).

To balance the various strengths and weaknesses of self-review and external review, a large and growing number of institutions combine internal and external review. In some institutions, a single review team—a mixed review group—is selected consisting of both internal and external reviewers. The external reviewers may include faculty from within or without the institution or both. The University of Illinois at Urbana/Champaign, for example, uses a mixed review group that includes program faculty and university faculty from outside the program being reviewed to review its programs.

A more common approach to internal/external program review is to use multiple reviews in which self-reviews and external reviews are conducted separately. At Trenton State College, two separate reviews are conducted—one self-review and one external review (the latter conducted by peer faculty from other institutions who are in the discipline or field being reviewed). In some institutions, three separate reviews are conducted. At the University of Arizona College of Education during the 1983–84 academic year, for example, a self-review by faculty in the college was followed by a review by a universitywide committee comprised of faculty from outside the college. Subsequently, a committee comprised of faculty in education from other universities conducted an external review.

Models for Evaluation
Along with the selection of program reviewers, the models used to evaluate programs are a critical aspect of program review. An evaluation model not only provides the overall

framework for evaluation but also gives shape to the research questions, organizes and focuses the evaluation, and informs the process of inquiry.

The models used in program review are seldom made explicit, but all institutions use some model or combination of models to guide their review efforts. These models are reflected in the guidelines developed by the central review committee or administrative group designing the review process and in the reviews themselves. Thus, evaluation models can be inferred from the guidelines and reports accompanying program reviews as well as from the literature on program review.

Based on their program review guidelines and practices, most institutions use various models for program evaluation, emphasizing one of four evaluation models: a goal-based model, a responsive model, a decision-making model, or a connoisseurship model. As displayed in table 2, this taxonomy draws heavily on the classifications of program evaluation models of several writers (Gardner 1977; Guba and Lincoln 1981; House 1978; Mines, Gressard, and Daniels 1982; Popham 1975). These models are discussed in the following paragraphs in terms of their focus and organizing principle, evaluation design, and application in an institutional setting.

Goal-based model

Grounded in the work of Tyler (1949), the goal-based approach to evaluation is the oldest and most widely used model of evaluation in higher education. Several alternative goal-based models have been introduced in the last several decades, but all goal-based evaluation is organized around the extent to which the program under review achieves its intended objectives (Craven 1980b, p. 436).

A goal-based model defines evaluation as the process of identifying program goals, objectives, and standards of performance, using various tools to measure performance, and comparing the data collected against the identified objectives and standards to determine the degree of congruence or discrepancy (Gardner 1977, pp. 577–78). In this model, the most important components of the evaluation design are the identified goals, objectives, and criteria used to judge relative success or failure. Decisions about measurement and interpretation are normally left in the hands of

TABLE 2

A TAXONOMY OF EVALUATION MODELS

Model	Proponents[a]	Model Organizer	Evaluation Questions
Goal-based Model	Tyler 1949 (Behavioral Objectives) Provus 1971 (Discrepancy Model) Popham 1975	Goals and objectives	To what extent is the program achieving its objectives?
Responsive Model	Scriven 1973 (Goal-free Model) Stake 1975 (Responsive Model) Parlett and Deardon 1977 (Illuminative Evaluation Model) Guba and Lincoln 1981 (Naturalistic Responsive Model)	Concerns and issues of stakeholders	What are the activities and effects of the program? What does the program look like from a variety of perspectives?
Decision-making Model	Stufflebeam et al. 1971 (Context-Input-Process-Product Model) Alkin 1972 (UCLA Center for the Study of Evaluation Model) Alkin and Fitz-Gibbon 1975	Decision making	To what extent is the program effective? In light of alternative decisions, what is the worth of the program?
Connoisseurship Model	Eisner 1975 (Connoisseurship Model)	Critical review by connoisseurs	How do critics interpret and evaluate the programs?

[a]Evaluation models associated with particular individuals are indicated in parentheses.

those individuals actually conducting the evaluation, although final judgments about merit and worth of the program usually are made by those overseeing the evaluation.

While all goal-based models place major emphasis on assessing the degree of congruence between objectives and performance, a goal-based approach need not focus exclusively on the extent to which goals and objectives are met. In the Provus (1971) model, for example, attention also is placed on describing and interpreting program performance and on exploring the reasons for relative success or failure. Thus, a goal-based process can have a formative role (evaluation aimed at improving a program) as well as a summative one (evaluation of a program for purposes of making a decision about the program) (Worthen and Sanders 1973, pp. 63–65). Still, as employed in academic program reviews, most goal-based evaluations seem to be predominantly summative: Designing an evaluation that will provide a foundation for making decisions about a program (resource allocation and program continuance, for example) is emphasized.

The design of goal-based evaluation may vary from simple to complex but invariably includes the following elements:

- clarification of the goals and objectives of the program under review
- identification of the factors or variables affecting performance
- delineation of the criteria and standards against which program performance will be assessed
- development of techniques and procedures for collecting data on performance
- data collection
- comparison of the data with the previously identified criteria and standards, leading to a judgment of worth
- communication of the findings (Gardner 1977, p. 578).

As the major approach to evaluation in higher education, the goal-based model drives academic program review in hundreds of colleges and universities. A good example of the approach is the evaluation system used at Broome Community College in Binghamton, New York. Adapted from the model of program evaluation for two-year colleges called Reality-Based Evaluation (RBE) for Two-Year Occupational Programs (developed by the Cornell Institute for Research and Development in Occupational Education), this model aims to improve decision making in areas such as goals, standards, and program expansion or curtailment. As implemented at Broome Community College, the RBE model is a prototypical example of the goal-based approach. The evaluation model encompasses three general phases. The first phase attempts to clarify program objectives and activities, the second phase involves gathering information from a variety of sources to examine the extent to which program objectives are being met, and the third phase focuses on data analysis and overall interpretation of the findings. A written report describes all three phases of the review and presents recommendations (Barak 1982, pp. 105–7).

As the major approach to evaluation in higher education, the goal-based model drives academic program review in hundreds of colleges and universities.

Responsive model

In the last few years, a sharply contrasting approach to the goal-based model has been developed that has had considerable influence on program review practices at many institutions. The responsive model finds its roots in the goal-free model of Scriven (1972, 1973), although it has gone beyond his formulation. Briefly, Scriven took issue with the widely accepted notion that goals and objectives should drive the evaluation. He argued that "unintended effects" or "side effects" are often as important as intended effects. Scriven's goal-free model of evaluation was aimed at judging the effects of programs independent of what the effects were intended to be. In essence, Scriven's organizer for evaluation became "effects" rather than goals and objectives (Guba and Lincoln 1981, p. 17).

Building upon Scriven's contention that program goals and objectives should not drive program evaluation, Stake (1975) developed the responsive model; a number of other writers (Guba and Lincoln 1981; Parlett and Deardon 1977) supported and further developed this approach. In this model, evaluation focuses more on program activities than on the program's stated goals and objectives and is organized around the "concerns and issues of stakeholding audiences" (Guba and Lincoln 1981, p. 23).

To emphasize evaluation issues *that are important for each particular program, I recommend the* responsive evaluation *approach. It is an approach that trades off some measurement precision in order to increase the usefulness of the findings to persons in and around the program. . . . An educational evaluation is* responsive evaluation *if it orients more directly to program activities than to program intents; responds to audience requirements for information; and if the different value perspectives present are referred to in reporting the success and failure of the program* (Stake 1975, p. 14).

Thus defined, responsive evaluation can serve many different purposes: to serve as a tool for decision making, to improve understanding, to facilitate program improvement, and so on. The needs met by a given evaluation, however, are determined by the "different purposes and information needs of different audiences" (Stake 1975, p. 15). In program review, for example, the evaluation is shaped by concerns expressed by different audiences, such as administrators, students, program faculty and staff, and faculty from outside the program.

Responsive evaluation, then, is a process of collecting, analyzing, and interpreting information about a program in light of the concerns and issues of audiences that have a stake in the evaluation. Accordingly, program goals and objectives may or may not be centrally important to the issues identified or to the strengths and weaknesses of the program relative to those issues. Instead, all aspects of the program under review are taken into consideration relative to audience-defined issues, and "no single element (whether goals, resources, processes, or participants) is preconceived as being necessarily more important to the evaluation than another" (Gardner 1977, p. 584).

A responsive evaluation cannot be designed fully before the actual evaluation, however, inasmuch as each step is determined in part by its predecessors (Guba and Lincoln 1981, p. 36). These steps, which should not be carried out serially, include:

1. interviewing clients, program staff, and concerned audiences
2. limiting program scope

3. surveying program activities
4. discovering stated and real purposes of the program and the concerns of various audiences
5. conceptualizing issues and problems
6. identifying data needs based on identified issues
7. selecting observers and judges
8. collecting data
9. preparing portrayals and case studies based on "themes"
10. matching issues to audiences
11. presenting findings (Stake 1975).

To be sure, few (if any) colleges and universities have systematically applied the responsive model in their program reviews, but this model clearly has appeal to institutions that believe traditional approaches—especially the goal-based model—suffer limitations. As a result, some institutions have combined various aspects of the responsive model with other approaches to evaluation. The academic review process at the University of Colorado–Boulder, for example, is coordinated by an Academic Program Review Committee and consists of three stages: (1) a self-study conducted by the program under review; (2) an internal review by a committee of Boulder faculty and students from fields outside the program under review; and (3) an external review by disciplinary experts. In a manner consistent with the responsive approach to evaluation, the perspectives of several constituencies are sought. For example, the self-study committee consults the college dean early in the review process, students are surveyed during the self-study process, and faculty views are solicited during the preparation of the self-study report. Further, the internal review team interviews a representative group of faculty members and students, and the external review committee does extensive interviewing (University of Colorado–Boulder n.d.). The solicitation of views from all those constituencies connected to a program is characteristic of most evaluation processes in higher education and is a central tenet of the responsive model.

Decision-making model
Within the last several years, especially at institutions where academic program reviews are conducted to reallo-

cate resources or to decide whether a program should be continued, considerable interest has been evinced in using the decision as the major organizer for evaluation. In the decision-making model, neither goals and objectives (the goal-based model) nor the concerns and issues of various stakeholders (the responsive model) are necessarily a central component in the design of the evaluation.

Two prototypical decision-making models are the Context-Input-Process-Product (CIPP) model (Stufflebeam et al. 1971) and the UCLA Center for the Study of Evaluation (CSE) model (Alkin 1972). Both models are nearly identical in their major characteristics: The CIPP model defines evaluation as "the process of delineating, obtaining, and providing useful information for judging decision alternatives" (Stufflebeam et al. 1971, p. 40), whereas the CSE model defines it as "the process of ascertaining the decision areas of concern, selecting appropriate information, and collecting and analyzing information in order to report summary data useful to decision makers in selecting among alternatives" (Alkin 1972, p. 12).

Evaluation in the decision-making model is conducted for purposes of decision making and accountability; the CIPP model is built on the premise that information must be useful to decision makers. Evaluation is viewed as a cyclical, continuing process in which a formal "feedback mechanism provides for continuing assessment of decision-information needs and the obtaining and providing of information to meet those needs" (Gardner 1977, pp. 580–81).

A central feature of the CIPP model is that different types of decisions require varying kinds of information and hence different types of evaluation activities. Four types of evaluation have been identified, each corresponding to a different type of decision: (1) *context evaluation,* which assists decision makers in determining goals and objectives; (2) *input evaluation,* which assists decision makers in clarifying alternative ways of achieving program goals and objectives; (3) *process evaluation,* which provides feedback to decision makers; and (4) *product evaluation,* which provides decision makers with information as to whether a program should be continued, modified, or terminated (Stufflebeam et al. 1971, pp. 80–84). In the CIPP model, only context evaluation is an ongoing process. Input, process, and product evaluations are initiated only when the context evaluation points to a problem, need, or opportunity (Guba and Lincoln 1981, p. 15).

The design is the same for all four types of evaluation encompassed in the CIPP model, and it has three separate elements: delineating, obtaining, and applying. Delineating involves focusing the evaluation by identifying the decision situations to be served and defining the criteria to be used by decision makers in assessing alternatives, obtaining simply refers to collecting and processing the pertinent information, and applying refers to analyzing the data and reporting the findings to decision makers (Worthen and Sanders 1973, p. 144). In short, evaluation in the CIPP model is a process of delineating, obtaining, and applying information to the needs of decision makers.

While the CIPP model has not been widely employed in higher education, a growing number of institutions have initiated decision-oriented program evaluations. These evaluations are structured to meet administrative information needs by providing relevant and timely information. A good case in point is the University of Houston central campus, which has implemented a systematic, decision-oriented program evaluation system aimed at providing a foundation for allocating and reallocating funds among academic departments. While departmental resource needs ("relative resource consumptiveness") and program centrality are considerations in this model, the most essential element is ongoing qualitative evaluation of departments and programs. Through a complex series of matrices, the University of Houston has designed a system in which relevant information about academic programs is provided to campus administrators to facilitate decision making about the distribution of campus resources (Munitz and Wright 1980, pp. 31–38).

Connoisseurship model
In contrast to the first three models, Eisner's connoisseurship model (1975) represents a strikingly different approach to evaluation—one that a substantial number of institutions have used, at least in part, to guide academic program reviews. At first glance, this model may appear orthogonal to the other three: It also necessarily emphasizes the role of the program reviewer or evaluator. Yet in several important respects the model differs markedly from the other

models. First, and most important, the catalyst for evaluation is not the constellation of goals and objectives, not the concerns and issues of stakeholders, not decision making, but the connoisseur. Second, the model uses the human being (connoisseur) as the primary instrument of measurement (to some extent, also true with the responsive model). In turn, data collection, analysis, and interpretation are guided primarily by the connoisseur rather than the evaluation design and are less open to direct inspection than in the other models. Third, the connoisseurship model is based more on a metaphoric approach to evaluation (Guba and Lincoln 1981, p. 19).

As defined by Eisner, a connoisseurship model is based on two concepts drawn from the domain of art criticism: *educational connoisseurship* and *educational criticism*. Like works of art, education is highly complex, requiring "connoisseurship," or the "art of perception that makes such complexity possible" (Eisner 1975, p. 1). Because of his training and background, the connoisseur is by definition the individual best able to appreciate the subtleties and nuances of what he encounters.

> *If connoisseurship is the art of appreciation, criticism is the art of disclosure. What the critic aims at is not only to discern that character and qualities constituting the object or event [but also to provide] a rendering in linguistic terms of what it is he or she has encountered so that others not possessing his level of connoisseurship can also enter into the work. . . . The function of criticism is educational. Its aim is to lift the veils that keep the eyes from seeing by providing the bridge needed by others to experience the qualities and relationships within some area of activity. . . . The critic must talk or write about what he has encountered; he must . . . provide a rendering of the qualities that constitute that work, its significance, and the quality of his experiences when he interacts with it* (Eisner 1975, p. 1).

In a connoisseurship model, the evaluation is structured in accordance with the expectations of those served by the evaluation. In turn, the connoisseur may well be expected to consider guidelines and criteria. The evaluation, however, is structured basically around interaction between the connoisseur and the program under review, with few a priori constraints. As a result, the standards and criteria that connoisseurs use in reaching their judgments derive primarily from their experience as professionals and upon the collective experience of the profession (House 1978). In short, the judgment of the professional is accepted on the basis of both that individual's assumed superior knowledge and expertise, which accompanies his stature in the particular field in question, and a commonly shared value system (Gardner 1977, p. 574).

In the connoisseur model, then, the connoisseur alone guides the evaluation. Operating with few constraints, the evaluator is initially a processor of information, collecting data in whatever way he prefers—for example, documents, interviews, or observation. At the same time, however, he is constantly judging the program under review—sifting through the evidence, weighing relevant data, seeking to understand the "character" and "qualities" of the program, and fleshing out deeper meaning—in much the same way that the art critic judges a work of art. At the point of closure, the values and criteria that inform his judgments may or may not be fully disclosed, but whether left implicit or made explicit, the final report is based on the subjective judgments emanating from the connoisseur's own thought processes (Gardner 1977, p. 575), on his own construction of social reality.

One institution integrating the connoisseurship model into its overall approach to academic program review is the University of Nebraska–Lincoln (UN–L). At UN–L, the Academic Planning Committee, a faculty-dominated, campuswide committee, oversees the evaluation of all instructional and noninstructional programs on a five-year cycle. While a goal-based approach to self-study marks the initial step in the design of the evaluation, the key component of the review is the visit of the review team (Seagren and Bean 1981, p. 22). The typical review team includes a student from the department, a facilitator from the university's Office of Program Review, a UN–L faculty member from outside the department under review, and two external members (one to serve as chair) of the discipline under review.

While its review team is not entirely comprised of "connoisseurs," UN–L's approach is consonant with the con-

Whether left implicit or made explicit, the final report is based on the subjective judgments emanating from the connoisseur's own thought processes.

noisseurship model. Not only is the review team made up primarily of professionals-qua-connoisseurs; it is also given few guidelines and criteria that might constrain its efforts to explore the status and function of the program within UN–L and to assess program quality. Moreover, in language highly compatible with the connoisseurship model, the review team is encouraged to provide a "vision of both what the department is, or seems to be, and what it could be, given its qualities and the constraints [that] will affect its future development" (Seagren and Bean 1981, p. 25). With the review team as the central component in the review process, UN–L clearly has integrated several elements of the connoisseurship model into its program review process.

Evaluative Criteria

Nearly all colleges and universities involved in academic program review use evaluative criteria to some degree. To be sure, some institutions employ models, such as the connoisseurship or responsive approaches, that in theory reject the use of a priori criteria. In practice, however, virtually all institutions predetermine criteria to guide their program reviews.

Most institutions use similar evaluative criteria. While institutions may use different nomenclature and only infrequently use exactly the same criteria, an "essential sameness" pervades the general criteria used in reviews. Table 3 shows the most common evaluative criteria identified in the literature (Barak 1982; Blackburn and Lingenfelter 1973; Melchiori 1980; Shirley and Volkwein 1978) and in the sample of institutions used for this monograph. Although all institutions do not use all six of the subcriteria listed under "quality" in table 3, we know of no institution involved in program review that does not identify quality as a central criterion for evaluation. Furthermore, a majority of institutions use criteria related to need, demand, and program cost, though these criteria are used less frequently in those institutions where only internal or self-reviews are conducted.

While overall evaluative criteria are quite similar across postsecondary institutions, the number, specificity, and relative weight assigned to the criteria are markedly

TABLE 3
CRITERIA FOR EVALUATION IN
ACADEMIC PROGRAM REVIEWS

Quality
- Quality of faculty
- Quality of students
- Quality of curriculum
- Quality of support services (library, laboratories and equipment, physical plant, computer facilities)
- Financial resources
- Quality of program administration

Need
- Centrality to mission and other campus programs
- Value to society

Demand
- Present and projected student demand
- Demand for graduates

Cost
- Cost effectiveness
- Nonpecuniary costs and benefits

diverse. (As the next section discusses, the methods and techniques used to measure various criteria are also diverse.) Several institutional examples illustrate this diversity.

As part of a program review process mandated by the Kansas Board of Regents, the University of Kansas reviews each of its programs every four years. The major purposes of the reviews are to inform the board about institutional offerings, to improve management, to identify strengths, and to describe steps that can be taken to correct deficiencies. The criteria used to guide the reviews include enrollment trends, consistency of the program's objectives with institutional objectives, curricular strengths and weaknesses, qualifications and responsibilities of the faculty and staff, students' characteristics and qualifications, special support requirements, and program need (Kansas Board of Regents 1984).

At Ohio State University, quality is the major criterion for evaluation, but attention is given to other criteria, such as the effective use of resources and the value of the program. The criterion of value refers to such factors as the market for program graduates, the contribution of the program to the university's instructional program, and the relationship of program goals to societal needs (Office of Academic Affairs/Graduate School 1978).

At Southern Illinois University at Edwardsville, five major criteria are suggested for use in reviews of graduate programs: quality of instruction and learning, quality of faculty, centrality of the program, program value and/or uniqueness, and potential. While the same five criteria are employed across all program reviews, however, the relative weight assigned to each criterion may vary by program. The relative weight (a numerical score) assigned to each criterion is determined through negotiation between administrators of each program under review and the appropriate review committee. Thus, depending on program objectives, the relative importance placed on the various criteria may vary. For example, the rating criteria used to assess one program might emphasize quality of instruction and program centrality; for another program, greater emphasis might be placed on quality of the faculty and program potential (Russo, Brown, and Rothweiler 1977, pp. 293–94).

Methodological Approaches
Probably the most controversial aspect of designing academic program reviews concerns the methods used to evaluate programs. At least partly as a consequence of this controversy, institutions frequently employ a combination of methods and techniques. Nevertheless, the majority of colleges and universities emphasize either quantitative or qualitative methods that, in turn, are associated with quantitative and qualitative approaches to evaluation.

Table 4 compares the quantitative and the qualitative approaches to program review. Neither the table nor the following discussion should be taken to suggest that these two approaches are mutually exclusive, much less mutually antagonistic. Rather, quantitative and qualitative approaches can complement each other, and many institutions combine the two approaches in their reviews. Moreover, while the table and the discussion identify various characteristics to distinguish the two approaches, these

TABLE 4
COMPARISON OF QUALITATIVE AND
QUANTITATIVE APPROACHES
TO PROGRAM REVIEW

	Quantitative	Qualitative
Predominant Use	Summative Evaluation (decision making and accountability)	Formative Evaluation (program improvement)
Evaluation Models	Goal-based Model Decision-making Model	Responsive Model Connoisseurship Model
Orientation and Emphases	Hypothetic-Deductive Verification Objective Scientific Quantification Fixed Design Statistical Analysis	Inductive Discovery Subjective Naturalistic Description and Interpretation Emergent Design Holistic Analysis
Methodological Approach	Scientific Method	Naturalistic Inquiry Ethnography Participant Observation Grounded Theory Ethnomethodology
Methodological Techniques	Questionnaires Tests Records Unobtrusive Measures (objective indicators)	Personal Observation Interviews Field Study Documents Records Unobtrusive Measures

Source: Adapted from Conrad 1982; Glaser and Strauss 1967; Guba and Lincoln 1981; House 1978; Mims 1978; Patton 1980, 1981, 1982; Rogers and Gamson 1982; Rossi and Freeman 1982; Weiss 1972.

characteristics do not fall within the exclusive domain of either approach. For example, while the goal-based model is commonly associated with the quantitative approach, many institutions use a goal-based approach to evaluation that relies on qualitative as well as quantitative methods. Therefore, the characteristics identified with each approach should be viewed only as representing differences in orientation and emphasis.

Quantitative evaluation has a long history in higher education and is the most widely used approach today. Accreditation, for example, has historically emphasized quantitative measurement of program quality; similarly, program reviews at the state and institutional levels have emphasized quantitative techniques. Briefly, the quantitative approach is based on the natural science paradigm of hypothetic-deductive methodology, in which the scientific method is adapted to program evaluation. In the quantitative approach, the evaluative criteria or variables are identified and quantitative measures for those variables selected. The repertoire of quantitative measures includes questionnaires, tests, records, and objective indicators.

As applied in academic program reviews, criteria and standards are identified in design of the evaluation. As discussed previously, these criteria usually include such factors as cost, demand, need, and quality. In turn, one or more measures or indicators are selected for each criterion. For example, three frequently used quantitative measures of program demand include number of program graduates per year, number of majors in a program, and program credit-hour production. Because some criteria lend themselves better than others to quantification, institutions using a quantitative approach sometimes choose their criteria in concert with their selection of quantitative measures.

An example of an institution that uses quantitative information extensively in evaluation is San Mateo Community College, which has developed a three-phase process for evaluating academic and occupational programs. The first phase is an efficiency study involving a review of program enrollments over two years and a proxy measure for the program's income and expenditures. This proxy is the ratio of faculty contact hours per year (expenditures) to weekly student contact hours (revenue). A unit that falls below a specified threshold on either measure becomes a candidate for a Phase II review. The District Program Review Committee coordinates the Phase II review and collects both quantitative and qualitative data: student flow, market demand, course retention rates, cost analyses, faculty survey results, facility inventory, course scheduling practices, and program quality. After reviewing these data, the committee recommends areas for improvement. "If problems are not remedied within one year, the program will enter a Phase III review, an administrative recommendation to retain, consolidate, or eliminate the program" (Smith 1981, p. 2).

At the University of North Dakota, the graduate school has established a departmental self-evaluation procedure that places primary evaluative responsibility for graduate programs within the departments and relies heavily on quantitative information. As part of each review, a two-page, quantitative summary of significant trends is developed and a survey of program graduates conducted. This information is provided to each department and is used to respond to several aspects of a questionnaire that the graduate school has prepared. The graduate school also surveys all faculty members in a program and may, if deemed necessary, appoint an external review committee to help with the evaluation (University of North Dakota 1983).

In marked contrast, the qualitative approach to evaluation draws from a variety of epistemological and methodological traditions. The qualitative approach plants its roots most solidly in the traditions of ethnography and field study in anthropology (Pelto and Pelto 1978) but also draws from a variety of other perspectives, including phenomenology, symbolic interactionism (Denzin 1978), ethnomethodology (Garfinkel 1967), and ecological psychology (Barker 1968). In turn, a like diversity of qualitative methods exists: naturalistic inquiry, ethnography, and grounded theory.

While methodological differences clearly exist between the various qualitative evaluation strategies, all qualitative methods are holistic-inductive in that the evaluator seeks to generalize about the program under review within its natural setting. Unlike the quantitative approach, in which the design and evaluation criteria are determined in advance and guide data collection and analysis, the qualitative approach normally does not predetermine what variables are worth measuring. Instead of gathering quantitative data through predetermined scales or indicators, the qualitative researcher remains open to whatever emerges from the data.

> *In contrast to [the quantitative approach that measures] the relationships among a few carefully selected and narrowly defined variables, the holistic approach to research design gathers data on any number of aspects of the setting under study in order to assemble a complete picture of the social dynamic of the particular situation or program. This means that, at the time of data collection, each case, event, or setting under study is treated as a unique entity, with its own particular meaning and its own constellation of relationships emerging from and related to the context within which it exists* (Patton 1982, pp. 9–10).

As the qualitative inquiry progresses and as patterns emerge from the data, the evaluator constantly moves back and forth between the discovery of underlying patterns and the verification of those patterns, thereby gradually weaving a tapestry intended to provide a holistic interpretation of the program.

Especially under field conditions, qualitative inquiry replaces the "static snapshots" of the quantitative approach with a process-oriented approach to evaluation. Accordingly, qualitative researchers rely most heavily on personal observation and interviews but may also use records, correspondence, and other unobtrusive measures. Hence, in qualitative inquiry, qualitative data may:

> *consist of detailed descriptions of situations, events, people, interactions, and observed behaviors; direct quotations from people about their experiences, attitudes, beliefs, and thoughts; and excerpts or entire passages from documents, correspondence, records, and case histories* (Patton 1982, p. 5).

These data provide the raw material for program evaluation as the evaluator seeks to construct his nonquantitative portrayal of a program through the process of qualitative inquiry.

No evidence suggests that any institutions use a purely qualitative approach to evaluation, but most use it in part. The use of external evaluators by the California State University at Long Beach illustrates well the qualitative technique (Office of the Associate Vice President n.d.). At that institution, evaluators perform a variety of functions, one of the most important being to synthesize a variety of information and provide a general assessment of a program that is based as much on experience and judgment as it is on quantitative indicators. Another frequently used qualitative technique is the internal review team. At the University of Pittsburgh, an internal review team comprised of university faculty is a central feature of that institution's process for evaluating graduate programs. The qualitative aspect of the team's work relates to the meetings held with administrators, faculty, and students connected to a program and to the discussions held with the external review team. Such meetings are considered to be essential if good judgments are to be made about such matters as a program's responsiveness to change, quality of theses, preeminence of the faculty, and program strengths (University Council 1980). It would be difficult to make judgments about these dimensions with quantitative measures alone.

MAJOR ISSUES IN PROGRAM REVIEW

Six issues concern the individuals in colleges and universities who are involved in academic program review: (1) accommodating multiple purposes; (2) selecting an evaluation model; (3) assessing quality; (4) using external reviewers; (5) increasing use of evaluations; and (6) assessing the impact of evaluations. (The selection of these six issues was based on two considerations—the significance of the issue and the extent to which a review of the literature might aid in illuminating its dimensions.) This chapter defines and clarifies these issues and presents alternative perspectives regarding their resolution. Those engaged in program review need to address these issues regularly.

Accommodating Multiple Purposes

Because a number of reasons usually exist for establishing a program review, institutions have developed a fairly lengthy list of purposes to guide their review efforts. The following list represents those adopted by many institutions:

- to assess program quality, productivity, need, and demand
- to improve the quality of academic offerings
- to ensure wise use of resources
- to determine the program's effectiveness and to consider possible modifications
- to facilitate academic planning and budgeting
- to satisfy state-level review requirements.

The advantage of designing an evaluation system that incorporates all of these purposes is that it will appeal to several constituencies. Such support is often needed in the early stages of implementation, but it can become self-defeating. It is possible, however, to design an evaluation system in which information is collected and judgments made that respond to widely different expectations.

Serious questions can be raised about two accommodations of purposes. The first involves institutional efforts to combine program improvement and resource reallocation as major purposes of the review. The second concerns an institution's attempts to use a single review process to satisfy both its own review agenda and that of a state-level coordinating or governing board.

Combining program improvement with resource reallocation
Although many institutions conducting program reviews
emphasize either the improvement of program quality or
resource reallocation (including program discontinuance), a
growing number of institutions combine both emphases
into a single process. At first glance, the two purposes
would seem compatible. Each requires an assessment of
current quality to identify where strengths exist and where
improvement is warranted. Most people also would agree
that quality assessment is an important first step in deciding how to reallocate resources. The problem, however, is
that it is difficult, if not impossible, for those responsible
for the review process to achieve both objectives at once.
"Quality assessment should not be ignored in a retrenchment process, but the two distinct motivations of improvement and reduction in resources will generally involve
somewhat different processes and may produce quite different results" (George 1982, p. 45). Several distinct difficulties in merging these two purposes merit consideration.

A major problem in attempting to achieve both purposes in
a single review system is that the underlying assumptions and
ultimate objectives may not be easily reconciled, if at all.
When an institution wishes to assess the quality of its programs and to improve programs where weaknesses appear,
the emphasis of the evaluation will be on how to assess current performance, on what progress has been made over
time, and on what institutional strategies might facilitate further improvement. At the University of North Carolina–
Asheville, for example, program improvement, not resource
allocation, was the principal incentive behind recent program
reviews. After studying a range of data, nine department
chairs rated the institution's programs on the basis of nine
criteria. Future resources of the institution were earmarked
for programs with low rankings to promote program
improvement (Cochran and Hengstler 1984).

On the other hand, the approach to evaluation is likely to
depart from this strategy if an institution concludes it must
reduce the number of program offerings or reallocate
resources away from low-priority or low-demand programs. In this case, evaluators must judge relative worth
and value and often must act quickly in the face of immediate budget pressures. In this situation, quality is only one
of several factors that gets considered.

In distinguishing between the two types of evaluations, it is useful to consider the "industrial" and "biological" models of evaluation (Pace 1972). The industrial model focuses on quantitative measures used to judge efficiency and productivity, and the biological model searches for ways to enrich experiences and to assess broader and more enduring program effects on students and society (Pace 1972). It is not stretching this analysis too far to suggest that most resource reallocation processes are frequently industrial in orientation, while program improvement processes are more biological. Others have questioned the compatibility of the two purposes, pointing out the great difference between a unit thinking it is being evaluated to identify areas needing additional strength and units thinking such an assessment serves to identify areas where quality is low and support should be diminished or even eliminated (Arns and Poland 1980).

The discussion of the review activities of the Select Committee on Academic Program Priorities at SUNY–Albany supports this view: "The Select Committee . . . felt a certain frustration that the budget recommendations had created a climate that led to the implementation of its negative recommendations but not its positive ones" (Volkwein 1984, p. 393).

Yet another problem in merging these two purposes is a temporal one: The careful assessment of quality and the development of recommendations for improvement require considerable time. Most institutions are unable to conduct more than six or eight program reviews each year. Such a protracted schedule does not mesh well with resource reallocation reviews, which usually transpire within relatively short periods in response to anticipated budget problems. The latter reviews use extant information on quality but usually lack sufficient time to conduct detailed analysis of the quality of every program offered. Hence, a timing factor militates against efforts to combine the two types of reviews.

Most resource reallocation processes are frequently industrial in orientation, while program improvement processes are more biological.

Accommodating institutional and state-level purposes
A second accommodation of purposes concerns how institutional review processes relate to the expectations for review of state higher education agencies. State agencies' authority and activity in program review have increased

dramatically in the last few years, and the proper role of
state boards in institutional review processes continues to
be debated.

A key issue in this debate is whether institutional and
state-level interests converge or are sufficiently complementary so that a single review process can achieve the
aims of both. Some believe that state-level interests can
indeed mesh with those of institutions (Hines 1980). In
Hines's view, the predominant institutional interest lies in
assessing merit, while state agencies are most interested in
statewide needs or plans. Although the primary objective
of review differs for the two groups, the secondary objectives overlap considerably; that is, states have more than
passing interest in merit, and institutions frequently want
to know how programs could be more responsive to statewide needs.

An analysis of the relationship between program review
for institutions and for state-level agencies identified eight
purposes for undertaking program reviews and discussed
how review responsibility varies by purpose (Wallhaus
1982) (see table 5, pp. 44–5). In this view, responsibility for
review is vested in the state agency when the review serves
to develop a statewide plan or overall programmatic priorities. Conversely, reviews focusing on curricular and personnel matters are the province of institutions. Between
these two extremes exist a number of purposes where the
assignment of responsibility is not so straight-forward. It is
these purposes that institutions and state agencies frequently try to accomplish cooperatively through a single
review process.

These cooperative efforts have been labeled ''shared
reviews'' (Floyd 1983). Responsibilities in shared reviews
are defined variously. Frequently, the institution conducts
the review and endeavors to attend to matters of interest to
both the institution and the state. On the surface, this plan
would seem to be reasonable and efficient. The issue,
again, is whether a single review process can have more
than one driving purpose.

In the last few years, a number of states have adopted
shared responsibilities for reviews. Illinois, Idaho, New
Mexico, California, Oregon, and Ohio have adopted review
processes in which the state agency, rather than conducting reviews itself, simply ensures that each institution is

doing so (Barak 1982). In a comparable arrangement within the University of Wisconsin system, each institution is required to have a review process and must report its findings to the system office (Craven 1980b). Only in unusual circumstances, such as when enrollments are low or when unnecessary duplication seems to exist, does the system office conduct a review of its own.

In shared reviews, then, institutions attempt to accommodate institutional and state-level purposes by developing an evaluation process that satisfies both institutional and state board requirements. In theory, the institution designs an evaluation system to meet its own needs and, by making minor adjustments in, say, data collection or reporting lines, is able to satisfy state-level needs as well. Moreover, this strategy minimizes duplication of review activities.

Despite these positive features, the shared review approach has drawn criticism. While combining reviews appears to be a solid idea, theoretical and practical reasons militate against the success of such an approach (Barak 1982, p. 84). For example, whereas institutions frequently establish the need for a program on the basis of students' or faculty members' perspectives, state agencies usually look at program need from a societal or manpower perspective. Another example of potential conflict centers on efficiency. Institutions tend to assess efficiency by comparing similar departments on campus or by collecting data from peer departments. State agencies tend to look at efficiency from a statewide perspective, for example, how costs in a discipline vary among institutions in the state. Thus, separate reviews by institutions and state agencies may be the best solution (Barak 1982, pp. 84–88).

Under certain conditions, combined reviews may not be productive (Wilson 1984). If the system office or state-level board prescribes the review process in too much detail, local initiatives aimed at establishing an effective system may be stifled. Where the state agency insists upon close adherence to a prescribed format, it may be more useful for separate reviews to be conducted, one by the institution for its own use, another by the state agency.

Selecting an Evaluation Model
The key issue for evaluators is which model—goal-based, responsive, decision-making, and connoisseurship—should

TABLE 5
PURPOSES AND OBJECTIVES OF PROGRAM REVIEW

	Tends to be more closely tied to state-level responsibilities	Tends to be more closely tied to institutional responsibilities
• Determination of statewide educational policies, long-range plans, and programmatic priorities (that is, support development of statewide master plans)	X	
• Elimination of unnecessary program duplication or, conversely, identification of needs for new programs	X	
• Determination of educational and economic priorities in terms of:		
1. consistency with role and mission	X	
2. need for improvement or expansion and additional resources necessary to accomplish (link to budget decisions)	X	
3. decisions to decrease or terminate (link to resource reallocation decisions)	X	
• Determination of relationship to established standards of quality, or preparation for entry into professions, and so on (link to accreditation, continuation of operating authority, or licensing authority)	X	
• Improvement of communications with constituents; assurance that information provided to students, prospective students, parents, alumni, governmental agencies, and others is consistent with actual practice	X	
• Determination of quality controls and policies (for example, admission policy, graduation requirements)		X

| | X |
| | X |

- Determination of curricular modifications, advisement procedures, institutional plans, and priorities relative to instructional, research, and service objectives

- Personnel and organizational decisions—faculty promotion and tenure, academic leadership, organizational structures, and philosophies

Source: Wallhaus 1982, p. 77.

guide program reviews in higher education, and the decision is an important one:

Where an administrator has a choice with regard to the type of evaluation to be conducted . . . that individual should be fully aware of the fundamentally different assumptions and outcomes that obtain when a particular type of strategy is selected (Gardner 1977, p. 572).

Goal-based model

The goal-based model focuses principally on assessing the extent to which a program's formal objectives are being achieved. As part of this effort, considerable attention is given to specifying program objectives, establishing standards of performance, identifying data to assess performance, and evaluating whether objectives have been achieved.

A goal-based approach to evaluation offers a number of positive features. First, the importance placed on objectives focuses attention on what those responsible for a program hope to accomplish. These goal statements become more than general statements of intent; they are specified as precisely as possible because of their significance to the subsequent assessment of performance. Second, a goal-based system can be used to make periodic checks of progress (formative evaluation) as well as to make consummate judgments of program worth (summative evaluation). Third, the approach encourages systematic attention not only to whether program goals have been reached but also to those features contributing to success or failure. For example, if the desired goal is to increase student retention and if certain actions are taken to achieve this goal, the goal-based design would require both an assessment of whether retention had improved and an understanding of the effect on retention of the actions themselves.

To be sure, the goal-based model has some limitations. The specification of goals can become an obsession resulting in lengthy lists covering every conceivable desire, significant as well as trivial, for a program. "Some people believe that when every objective is related to every other, the program is properly arranged" (House 1982, p. 10). But "a major criticism of evaluation as congruence between performance and objectives is that a focusing on measurable products rather than processes occurs. This may permit the overlooking of important side effects'' (Feasley 1980, p. 9). In essence, this criticism berates the propensity of evaluators to focus on whether goals have been accomplished while ignoring other, unintended contributions that goal statements have not captured.

On a related matter, the goal-based system has been criticized because of the inflexible way in which a priori goals drive the process (Guba and Lincoln 1981). Evaluators have a tendency to accept the goal statements and to pursue data relating to those goals in a very determined way. If, in mid-evaluation, it becomes apparent that some of the goal statements no longer apply or that those responsible for the program should change directions, the goal-based evaluator might not perceive the necessary changes or, more significantly, might not be inclined to suggest that plans be changed, even if the need is apparent. Thus, the goal-based model sometimes engenders a single-minded pursuit of information relating to goal statements while ignoring everything else.

Perhaps the major defect of the goal-based approach lies in its assumption that ways can be found to measure performance in relation to all goals. This observation is especially significant for those institutions of higher education in which goals, such as those of program quality or centrality, frequently are elusive. Attempts to "force" a goal-based model in a particular setting may result in redefining the goals in ways that can be measured (for example, number of publications equals research quality), thus trivializing what is being done.

Use of the goal-based model, therefore, offers the two advantages of a systematic attention to how a program has performed in relation to its intent and of a concern for the factors contributing to its success or failure. The model's chief limitations are the propensity to reduce everything to a goal statement, the insensitivity to outcomes that are unrelated to goal statements, and the assumption that valid measures can be found for all goals.

Responsive model
The driving objective of the responsive model is to collect information to illuminate the concerns and issues of those who have a stake in an evaluation. Program goals are not

central. In essence, a responsive evaluation investigates what various constituents believe a program is accomplishing and their concerns about the program.

The strength of this model is that it can help those responsible for a program to understand both its actual achievements and where action is needed to reconcile results with plans. For this reason, a responsive approach can be especially helpful during the early and middle stages of program implementation.

One major criticism of the responsive model is that it is "unscientific" and lacks an emphasis on formal measurement (Gardner 1977). Critics suggest that the role of the evaluator is not to observe a program from afar and to make judgments based on the analysis of "objective" data but to become immersed in the program to the point of rendering an accurate description and interpretation of its accomplishments. Such immersion, however, may well sacrifice objectivity, and it certainly increases the time commitment to a review.

One particular type of responsive evaluation—the case study—has some definite shortcomings: the fact that the evaluator assumes enormous responsibility in trying to portray a program accurately; the difficulty for the evaluator to protect against bias; the requirement for a large number of subjective judgments (House 1982).

Decision-making model

The main purpose of the decision-making model is to conduct evaluations responsive to the informational needs of decision makers. The strength of this model derives from the explicit connection between evaluation and decision making, a link that focuses the evaluation and increases the likelihood that results will be used.

"The principal criticism of the decision-oriented approach is that the evaluator accepts the decision context and values/criteria that have been defined by the decision makers" (Feasley 1980, p. 10). This criticism implies that the evaluator is aligned with the decision makers and may find it difficult to remain objective. The evaluator collects data according to the questions defined by decision makers and accepts the values implicit in their questions. If those responsible for the program do not share such values or consider the questions unimportant, the evaluation will not be credible.

Another problem is that this model assumes rational decision making (Gardner 1977). The task of the evaluator is to identify the questions of interest, collect pertinent information, present findings, and wait for the results to be used. The evaluation therefore becomes a critical ingredient in decision making. This approach is likely to overemphasize the importance of evaluative information and to fail to recognize that evaluations provide only one source of data for decision makers. Further, to assume that all decision alternatives can be accurately anticipated and that sufficient data can be collected in relation to these alternatives is to place unrealistic expectations on an evaluation.

Decision makers are frequently biased in their acquisition and processing of information (O'Reilly 1981, pp. 56–57), and this bias occurs in the search for information, in the preference for information that is easy to secure and supports preconceived ideas, in the transmission of information that distorts reality if it optimizes certain outcomes, in the selective use of available information, and in the preference for vivid examples, even if they are misleading.

A final criticism of this model relates to an evaluator's ability to identify decision makers. It is not easy to identify decision makers in many complex organizations (Guba and Lincoln 1981). Decisions are frequently made at several organizational levels, by various individuals. Most actions involve more than one decision maker and a number of key decision points. It is almost impossible to identify all of these individuals and to collect all of the data necessary to inform them.

Another problem is that this model assumes rational decision making.

Connoisseurship model

The central tenet of the connoisseurship model is that an expert (a connoisseur) can use his experience and expertise to judge a program. In essence, the human being is the measurement instrument.

The use of outside reviewers in higher education is a good example of the connoisseurship model. The strength of this model is that those who are most knowledgeable about a subject are asked to make the assessment. The connoisseurship model has high credibility because those within a discipline or profession are judged by peers who have a sound basis for understanding what is—or is not— being accomplished.

One problem is that the connoisseurship model frequently lacks evaluative guidelines, so that a premium is placed on the evaluator's judgment; it is hard to know whether the evaluator's perceptions are accurate (Guba and Lincoln 1981). Many institutions attempt to sidestep this problem by inviting more than one expert to participate in a review, a strategy introducing valuable "triangulation." At the same time, however, this strategy can yield as many different assessments as there are evaluators.

Another problem with this approach lies in the difficulty of generalizing across programs (Feasley 1980, p. 8). In rating different programs, no two experts will have the same value structure or will weigh criteria equally. One evaluator may rate a program weak because of difficulties in its graduate instructional program; another may overlook the graduate program entirely if the record of faculty research is strong.

The connoisseurship model is popular in higher education because most faculty members believe that only those within a discipline can adequately evaluate accomplishment. Certainly, a disciplinary background can greatly enhance an evaluation. At the same time, certain problems are inherent—the ability to generalize procedures across programs, the subjectivity of perceptions, and the emphasis placed on the person chosen to conduct the evaluation.

Assessing Quality
For those engaged in program review, the assessment of quality has generated more confusion and debate than any other issue. Pressure always has existed to define "quality" and to determine which types of information should be collected, but more recently, interest has burgeoned because of the emphasis on program review for reallocation and retrenchment. The problem is that no one has yet found a way to measure quality directly. The issue for evaluators is how to define this concept and how to determine what types of information (indicators) should be used to guide data collection.

The literature (cf. Astin 1980; Conrad and Blackburn *In press* b) and institutional documents identify four perspectives on how to define quality: a reputational view, a resources view, an outcomes view, and a value-added view. The particular view held affects the kind of information used to assess quality. The issue is which of these views of quality is most accurate and helpful (see table 6).

TABLE 6
VIEWS OF QUALITY AND
REPRESENTATIVE INDICATORS

Reputational View

- Peer judgments of the quality of program, students, faculty, or resources

Resources View

- Student selectivity
- Student demand
- Faculty prestige
- Faculty training
- Faculty teaching loads
- Budget affluence
- Library holdings
- Equipment adequacy
- Size of endowment

Outcomes View

- Faculty scholarly productivity
- Faculty awards and honors
- Faculty research support
- Faculty teaching performance
- Student achievement following graduation
- Student placement
- Student achievement
- Alumni satisfaction

Value-added View

- Change in students' cognitive abilities
- Student personal development
- Student career development
- Social benefits

Reputational view

This view of quality is derived from the connoisseurship model of evaluation and assumes that experts in the field make the best judgments on the criterion. In essence, the reputational view reflects a belief that the optimum way to assess quality is to seek a consensus of informed opinion. The typical indicator is some type of reputational survey. The past two decades have seen a number of surveys of this type (Cartter 1966; Jones, Lindzey, and Coggeshall 1982; Roose and Anderson 1970).

The main strength of this view lies in the fact that the raters are those who supposedly know best what quality is. It also has an intuitive appeal to ratings, reflecting what most people believe is true (Webster 1981).

Reputational rankings are criticized, however, because, while the raters may have insight into the scholarly productivity and reputation of a department, they are not likely to know much about the instructional program. Surely a program assessment must include more than research and scholarship (Conrad and Blackburn 1985). The lack of national visibility for many programs suggests that even reputational rankings based on faculty members' scholarly productivity are not likely to be meaningful below the top 15 or 20 programs in the country (Webster 1981). Other problems are apparent—"reputational lag" (the ranking of programs based on their quality several years ago) and "halo effects" (ranking a program high because the institution is held in high regard). These and other limitations are discussed extensively in the literature (Conrad and Blackburn 1985; Dolan 1976; Lawrence and Green 1980; Webster 1981).

Despite these limitations, such ratings have received support:

In our view controversy over reputational studies should not deter researchers from conducting such studies in the future. If reputational studies are designed to respond to the criticisms . . . we are persuaded that they can make an important contribution to the evaluation of quality in higher education (Conrad and Blackburn 1985, p. 23).

Resources view
This particular view of quality emphasizes the human, financial, and physical resources that go into a program. According to this view, high quality exists where these resources—bright students, excellent faculty, adequate budgets, strong research support, strong libraries, and adequate facilities—are plentiful. The extent to which these resources are available to a particular program has been measured in various ways—for example, student test scores, proportion of the faculty with a doctorate, grant support, and number of volumes in the library. The advantages of using such measures of resources are that relevant data are readily available at most institutions, that the measures reflect what exists today, not what the situation was a decade ago, and that comparisons can be made across all colleges and universities, not just a few highly ranked institutions (Webster 1981).

Notwithstanding these benefits, the resources view suffers some serious limitations. Little evidence supports the view that more resources equate with increased student learning (Astin 1980). Further, and more important, the resources approach places a false ceiling on the amount of quality that can exist in higher education by asserting that "such resources as bright students and prestigious faculty are finite" (Astin 1980, p. 4).

Outcomes view

Another way to define and assess quality is to emphasize results—what the investment of resources produces. Here, attention is focused on the quality of the product. Typical indicators associated with this view are faculty productivity, students' accomplishments following graduation, employers' satisfaction with program graduates, and institutional contributions to the solution of local, state, or national problems. Specific outcome measures include the number of faculty publications in scholarly journals, the number of graduates admitted to leading graduate or professional schools, employer surveys, percentage of graduates finding employment soon after graduation, and lifetime earnings of graduates.

Collecting information on outcomes boasts a number of advantages. Chief among them is the emphasis on what is happening to those who are or have been part of a program; the focus of attention shifts from the resources invested to the results. Like the resource measures, many of the outcomes measures hold relevance for all institutions; all institutions, for example, are interested in the accomplishments of their alumni (Webster 1981).

Perhaps the most significant problem with the outcomes view is the difficulty of delineating the special institutional contribution to results. "Most output measures depend more on the quality of students admitted to the institution than on the functioning of the institution or the quality of its program" (Astin 1980, p. 3). Another disadvantage is that outcomes measures frequently limit themselves to the past. The period between graduation and inclusion in *Who's Who in America* obstructs the drawing of precise conclusions about the current quality of a program (Webster 1981).

Value-added view

This view of quality focuses attention on program impact. "The basic argument underlying the value-added approach is that true quality resides in the institution's ability to affect its students favorably, to make a positive difference in their intellectual and personal development" (Astin 1980, pp. 3–4). Consonant with this view, evaluation should attempt to identify what a program contributes to students' learning. One typical indicator is what students learn while enrolled, which is sometimes measured by administering an achievement test at the time of enrollment and at graduation.

The chief advantage of this view is that one takes into account the quality of students at entry. This approach is especially attractive to institutions seeking to respond to "the twin doctrines of entitlement and equal education opportunity" (Lawrence and Green 1980, p. 54). Thus, institutions are judged by how much they help students, by how much they "add" to students' knowledge and personal development.

Like the other views of quality, the value-added approach has limitations. First, it is expensive, both in time and money. Investigating a program's contribution requires extensive recordkeeping for a large number of students. Another problem is the difficulty of reaching consensus on what students should learn and on measuring such quantities, even if they are defined (Lawrence and Green 1980, p. 40). For example, significant measurement problems are associated with assessing how much a student has improved in critical thinking skills. Finally, it is no easy matter to determine what one program's contribution is to a student's learning or development. The effects of other variables, such as maturation, travel experiences, and summer employment, are difficult to control.

Using External Reviewers

This review of current evaluation processes indicates that most institutions have incorporated the judgments of external reviewers into their program reviews. Most often, these reviewers are faculty members within the same discipline but at another institution or within the institution but outside the program under review. The issue faced by those designing an evaluation system is to decide which of these two types of reviewers to use. Knowledge of the possible strengths and limitations of each should prove helpful in making the choice.

Reviewers from other institutions

The use of peers from other institutions to help in institutional reviews is rapidly becoming the norm rather than the exception. The program review process at California State University at Long Beach illustrates the use of outside reviewers. That institution's review process consists of four phases: (1) a self-study prepared by those in the program under review; (2) a review by a subcommittee of faculty from other programs on campus; (3) an external review by disciplinary experts; and (4) a "response report" prepared by those in the program (Office of the Associate Vice President n.d.). The external review serves to provide a comparative perspective, which is balanced with the program's own view and that of colleagues on campus.

Like other approaches to assessing program quality, the use of external peers has its strengths and weaknesses. Characteristic of the problems are the following observations on experiences with outside reviewers at the University of Nebraska–Lincoln: The selection of a review team was frequently controversial; the review teams suffered because of lack of knowledge about the local context; too little time was available for the reviews; the review teams tended to focus on insignificant issues; the review teams often were asked to address problems they could not resolve; the review teams were provided with more information than they could comprehend; and the review teams tended to solve all problems by recommending additional resources (Seagren and Bean 1981, pp. 20–24).

In a more positive vein, the use of external peers provides a perspective that is frequently helpful. In most program reviews, it is considered crucial to have some kind of disciplinary perspective on the quality of what is being done and to seek advice on future directions. In addition, reports from external peers are usually perceived as objective and therefore can stimulate change that might not otherwise be possible.

Reviewers from the same institution

A number of institutions choose to use on-campus (but outside the discipline) colleagues to help evaluate programs.

At California State University at Long Beach, for example, faculty from within the institution conduct an internal review of a program to provide an assessment based on institutional (as opposed to disciplinary) standards of performance and quality (Office of the Associate Vice President n.d., Appendix B, p. 14). This strategy offers the advantages of familiarity with the local context and norms and a stake in the results. The recommendations will affect not only those evaluated but also the evaluators—they must live with what they recommend. On the other hand, such reviewers may frequently be unfamiliar with the discipline under study or, conversely, tend to allow previous familiarity with a program or its personnel to bias results.

Despite these criticisms, many believe that reviewers outside a particular discipline can recognize quality as long as enough information is available and enough opportunities exist to interact with program personnel. An interesting test of this idea examined results of faculty ratings of students' oral examinations (DiBiaso et al. 1981). A graduate school representative from outside the student's discipline was appointed to each of the review committees. A comparison of the ratings of the internal and external reviewers revealed

> *no evidence of a significant difference between how graduate school representatives rate examinations conducted inside their own colleges compared to their ratings of examinations outside their own colleges. These results suggest that members have some common perceptions about the quality of doctoral examinations, regardless of discipline* (DiBiaso et al. 1981, p. 10).

Thus, the issue is not whether to use reviewers in higher education, but whether to use on-campus colleagues or disciplinary peers.

Increasing Use of Evaluations

One of the most perplexing issues facing evaluators is how to increase the likelihood that others will employ the results of their efforts. Considerable time and attention is being given to evaluation these days, yet a frequent criticism is that the results of such efforts really have no effect on decisions. The perception is that evaluations are undertaken not because the results are expected to be used but because someone simply feels they "ought to be done." This criticism is so prevalent that it must be taken seriously.

To the uninitiated, it would seem that the issue of use should not even arise. Is not the basis of an evaluation the need for information to make a decision or to become more knowledgeable about a program or activity? If so, then every evaluation should be used. Nevertheless, utilization is a problem.

The results of program evaluations are not used for four general reasons: (1) organizational inertia; (2) the state of evaluation practice, for example, the inability to define valid measures of important criteria; (3) the uncertainty about the need for some evaluations; and (4) the multiple sources of information competing for the attention of decision makers (Anderson and Ball 1978).

The conflicting information needs of people at different levels of an organization make it difficult to conduct a useful evaluation (Patton 1985, p. 13). Highly detailed discussion of a specific case is seldom of much use at higher organizational levels; aggregate comparisons are of little use at the unit level. One important reason for lack of use of an evaluation is the inadequate personal involvement and commitment of key people. The personal factor is more crucial than structural, organizational, or methodological variables (Patton 1981, pp. 15–16).

Use of evaluations is also hindered because institutions compartmentalize the function of evaluation. Typically, the responsibility for program review is assigned to a staff office or to a specific individual. The delegation of responsibility for program review by the executive officers of an institution relieves them of the responsibility for such activities and places distance between those conducting the reviews and those in a position to use the results.

Utilization is also impeded because decisions frequently involve social, political, and financial considerations outside the task of evaluation. It should not be too disturbing to evaluators to know that occasionally these other considerations will outweigh the findings of an evaluation report (Dressel 1976; O'Reilly 1981).

Given that these problems exist, the issue of how to increase the likelihood that results will be used warrants special attention. This matter has engendered a number of

A frequent criticism is that the results of such efforts really have no effect on decisions.

views. Anderson and Ball (1978), for instance, recommend encouraging communication between those evaluated, those evaluating, and those responsible for the process; varying the modes for disseminating results according to audiences; identifying users early and finding ways to make sure that their questions are being addressed; finding ways to include those responsible for the evaluation in its planning; reporting results in a timely way; and maximizing such virtues as brevity, timeliness, and responsiveness. Others suggest that utilization should become an immediate rather than a postreport concern, that reports relate to the concerns of decision makers, that credibility and rapport be maintained, and that all participants in the evaluation communicate among themselves (Brown and Braskamp 1980). "Evaluation is undertaken in a social and political environment in which various groups have vested interests in the evaluation process. . . . If an evaluation is to be used by these groups in their deliberations, discussions, and policy making, the evaluation system must be designed to maximize communication among these audiences" (Braskamp 1982, p. 58).

A critical element in utilization relates to the approach of the evaluator (Alkin 1980). In particular, rapport established with program staff can enhance use of results. Use is not related to any particular evaluation model; the most important consideration is to adapt the strategy to the program and to the questions being asked.

One of the most important ways to increase utilization is for decision makers and information users to be clearly identified (Patton 1978). Decision makers cannot be treated as "abstract audiences" (p. 284). Decision makers should not delegate responsibility for an evaluation but should assume an active role in its implementation:

> *There has been considerable discussion in the literature and among evaluators about how to make managers, clinicians, board members, and others better consumers of evaluations. . . . This effort is misplaced. For evaluations to be useful and to be used, the managers have to accept responsibility for owning and defining the evaluation function* (Clifford and Sherman 1983, p. 32).

One way to increase use is to ensure that evaluators focus their efforts on three issues: (1) who the decision makers will be; (2) what information is needed; and (3) when the information is needed (Feasley 1980, p. 43). Perhaps the most important issue is to identify the evaluative question (Patton 1978).

A study of the characteristics of decision makers identifies six managerial characteristics relating to the issue of utilization:

1. Decision makers work at an unrelenting pace;
2. their daily routines are characterized by brevity, variety, and fragmentation;
3. they prefer active rather than passive use of time;
4. they prefer verbal as opposed to written communication;
5. they serve as active communication links;
6. they blend rights as well as duties so that personal objectives can be realized (Mintzberg 1973, chap. 3).

This list suggests that evaluations are more likely to be used if they relate to decision makers' concerns, are communicated clearly and concisely, and are presented both verbally and in written form.

In wrestling with the question of utilization, institutions have adopted several strategies to try to ensure that results of evaluations will somehow link to other decision-making processes. Ohio State University has developed the concept of a loosely coupled system, which means that all "parties to a review," including the college dean, the university's chief academic officers, the graduate dean, and those in the program, are consulted throughout the review process. At the conclusion of the review, a "memorandum of understanding" is developed in which the parties agree on actions to be taken. These agreements are monitored and updated each year (Arns and Poland 1980).

At the University of North Carolina at Asheville, six aspects of the program review process contribute to its usefulness:

1. clarity of purpose
2. involvement of decision makers in all stages of the process
3. maximization of communication

4. understanding of the political nature of the environment
5. recognition of the subjectivity of evaluation
6. competence of the institutional research staff and confidence in the data collected (Cochran and Hengstler 1984, p. 184).

At the State University of New York at Albany, evaluations are an integral part of a planning process. The evaluations consist of both annual monitoring of programs and five-year in-depth reviews. This arrangement is useful because:

1. *it capitalizes on an annual, synoptic view across all major university activities;*
2. *it is a goal-driven activity;*
3. *it is merged with resource allocation, thereby linking budgeting with evaluation;*
4. *evaluation (both ongoing annual monitoring as well as selected in-depth reviews) provides feedback for planning and resource allocation;*
5. *it more clearly integrates evaluation with existing decision-making structures and processes* (Hartmark 1982, p. 16).

Thus, a review of the literature on utilization reveals consensus on the objective of utilization but little agreement on how it is best accomplished, and suggestions vary from encouraging decision makers to participate more actively in evaluation to accounting for the managerial characteristics of decision makers to conducting evaluations in a manner responsive to those characteristics.

Assessing Impact

If results are used, another issue emerges—the impact of those results. The basic concern is whether the consequences of implementing an evaluation are positive or negative. First, however, one must distinguish between the outcomes and the effects of a review—a subtle but important distinction. Decisions to eliminate a program, to increase admissions requirements, to change department heads, or to establish consortia are outcomes, not effects, of program reviews. As defined here, "effect" refers to the consequences of actions taken. Concern about the effects therefore requires attention to the long-term effects of decisions, for example, whether the program is stronger, more efficient, or higher quality. Some believe the effects of program review are salutory; others are less optimistic. The question is which view is more correct.

How does one make such assessments? Efforts should focus on the question, "Does the system function better as a result of the evaluation effort?" (Cronbach 1977, p. 2). Explicit in this question is the principle that an evaluation must be beneficial.

The following kinds of consequences should be noted:

The ideal held forth in the literature is one of major impact on concrete decisions. The image that emerged in our interviews is that there are few major, direction-changing, decisions in most programming. . . (Patton 1978, p. 32).

Most conceptions are too narrow (Alkin 1980). Consequences cannot be examined solely on the basis of immediate impact; longer-term implications must also be considered. Evaluations have unintended results that go beyond the formally stated recommendations. Further, the evaluation process often generates benefits beyond those chronicled in a report. Thus, the assessment of impact must be done in a naturalistic way, as in conducting case studies and recording participant observations. Finally, one should not confuse lack of implementation with lack of impact. An evaluation report frequently provides valuable information even though no specific recommendations are implemented (Alkin 1980, pp. 21–22).

The assessment of impact must not be limited to immediate and direct influences; indirect, catalytic, and inclusive results also demand attention (Braskamp and Brown 1980, p. viii). This approach requires special skill in analyzing multiple causes of specific actions as well as a willingness to view utilization broadly. Thus, those assessing impact must heed results that may be latent as well as immediate, incremental as well as radical, subtle as well as obvious. This view of impact is consistent with the admonition that "most change in education is incremental rather than radical, and advertising of this fact would improve the climate for evaluation" (Dressel 1976, p. 5).

Just as the advice on how to assess impact is far from uniform, so too is the evidence on impact far from definitive. Most campuses have critics who believe that the costs of program review outweigh the benefits. Several criticisms have been cited frequently:

- Time and effort are wasted because more data are collected than can be productively used.
- Viewed as inherently threatening and negative, the review process creates unwarranted anxiety.
- Leaders' credibility is diminished because the information requested is not used, or its use is not made visible enough.
- Distrust is created because the uses of the information are not conceived and articulated clearly enough from the outset, confidentiality of the report is not clarified, or the various roles in the process are not adequately determined.
- Inaccurate information causes unwarranted embarrassment or pride.
- Attention and time are diverted from the institution's teaching, research, and service functions.
- Resentment arises because the process is not designed to be useful at the program level as well as at higher organizational or system levels.
- The review leads to raised expectations for resources that are unavailable, which causes disappointment (Seeley 1981, p. 56).

On the other hand, program review—"if implemented properly and combined with other retrenchment strategies—can be a major tool for effectively reducing expenditures while maintaining essential program quality" (Barak 1981, p. 219). A study of program reviews in research universities found, not surprisingly, that the benefits were greatest at the program level and least at the institutional level (Poulton 1978). Table 7 displays the nature of the effects at three organizational levels.

The results of graduate program reviews at the University of California indicated several conclusions: (1) the institutions conducting reviews did not save money and, in fact, lost money (if the cost of the review process itself is taken into account); (2) reviews did not uncover previously

TABLE 7
TYPICAL EFFECTS OF PROGRAM REVIEWS

Organizational Level	Relative Utility	Nature of Changes
Department/Program	Greatest Utility (primarily from single reviews)	• Increased introspection • Revised objectives for teaching and research • Better organized qualitative and quantitative information • Clarified unit/program goals, strengths, and deficiencies • Improved unit procedures • Improved contact among unit members • Improved rationale for resources • Potentially increased frustrations
School/College	Moderate Utility	• Improved information on unit trends and priorities, strengths, and weaknesses • Better indications of unit quality and responsiveness • Adjusted college policies and procedures • Adjusted resource decisions (occasional) • Adjusted organizational structures (occasional)
University Administration	Least Utility (requires accumulation of reviews)	• Revised institutional policies and procedures • Major organizational changes (rare) • Major budgetary commitments or cuts (rare)

Source: Adapted from Poulton 1978.

unknown information; (3) reviews did stimulate change in some situations; (4) the reviews did tend to clarify impressions and develop a fair portrayal of programs; and (5) many of the reviews' recommendations were implemented (Smith 1979, pp. 2–3). Overall, the study concluded that the institution benefited from the reviews. A similar assessment at the University of Iowa took place in 1977, when an ad hoc committee of the faculty senate was appointed to evaluate the program review process on campus (Barak 1982). Through interviews with participants, the committee found that the reviews required a substantial commitment of time and effort but that many positive benefits accrued to the institution. The self-study process was found to benefit the units and to lead to improvements. The reviews also provided systematic information useful in keeping faculty and administrators knowledgeable about programs.

A survey of the program review authority and practices of 37 state-level higher education agencies, paying special attention to results in terms of resources, found:

> *Despite the concern about resource savings, only one respondent supplied a dollar figure for resources saved. In fact, 95 percent of the 20 respondents who have discontinued programs do not know the amount of resources saved or reallocated and only 35 percent of those same 20 respondents believe that resources have been saved, even though they could not supply a dollar figure* (Skubal 1979, p. 231).

On the basis of these results, one of three possible scenarios is taking place: (1) savings accrued at the institutional level, rather than at the state level; (2) it was impossible to attach a dollar amount to the savings; and (3) the review activity was purely cosmetic—programs being eliminated involved no resources (Skubal 1979). As far as the state boards were concerned, program discontinuance had not had a substantial impact on resources (p. 232).

A study of the effects of program reviews conducted by state-level higher education agencies gave careful attention to the effects of the Louisiana Board of Regents' program reviews involving Louisiana State University–Baton Rouge (LSU) and Northeast Louisiana University (Mingle 1978). At LSU, no cost savings were realized, but the belief persisted that the reviews facilitated cooperation among programs, provided a basis for judging programs' worth and for reallocating resources, stimulated personnel changes, and enhanced quality standards. By contrast, the reviews at Northeast were viewed as biased and as having fostered a "sense of declining prestige and fear for the future" (p. 64).

Reviews conducted by the Florida Board of Regents used outside consultants to review selected programs in the nine universities of the system (Hill, Lutterbie, and Stafford 1979). The consultants' task was to review a particular program at all of the institutions and to make recommendations on "program quality, duplication of programs, financial support, and the need for any additional programs or a shifting of programs in the discipline under review" (p. 3). These reviews provided better documentation of the need for new programs, resulted in a small number of programs' being eliminated, and controlled program growth. Further, the reviews led to the establishment of several cooperative programs among institutions within the system and between those institutions and private colleges and universities in the state. For example, an engineering consortium was established, and contracts between the state and several private colleges and universities were developed. Further, the reviews helped the board identify underfunded areas and provided some systematic information that could serve as part of a recently initiated planning exercise (pp. 5–8).

While several problems with the review process were noted in Florida, the overall assessment was quite positive. The consultants' reports were believed to have aided greatly in identifying the strengths and weaknesses of programs in the system and in stimulating plans to strengthen some programs and to address important issues in others. "Some of the impact [of the reviews was] felt immediately by the universities, but the larger impact [was] more subtle as the intricate process of change in a multicampus system [was] initiated, developed, and brought to conclusion" (p. 9).

Although some evidence suggests that program reviews are helpful, the basis for this conclusion is weak, because only a few studies have examined effects systematically. Some evidence also suggests that such reviews do not achieve desired results. The stubborn fact is that not much is known about the effects of program review.

PROPOSALS FOR IMPROVING PROGRAM REVIEW

This chapter offers some tentative proposals on ways to improve program review processes, both as a practical guide and as a research agenda. For practitioners, the proposals suggest solutions to some recurring problems, drawing heavily on available research and institutional experiences. For researchers, the proposals constitute a set of hypotheses that need to be tested to determine their validity and utility. The proposals address a few important concerns rather than burying the significant among the pedestrian in a more comprehensive list of suggestions. The proposals relate to three general aspects of program review: purposes, processes, and results.

Purposes

1. Campus-based reviews should have a single driving purpose that is widely accepted and understood. Multiple purposes can be achieved only to the extent that their underlying assumptions and objectives are mutually supportive.

Many institutions have established review processes that encompass a broad range of purposes. These purposes often address fundamentally different objectives, and the success of reviews may be compromised if they are pursued simultaneously. A good illustration of inherent conflict can be found in reviews that seek both program improvement and resource reallocation.

It is difficult to sustain a review process with conflicting purposes (Barak 1982; George 1982). The root of the problem is often that the purposes of a review evolve in subtle ways. As the process is being developed, reviewers are inclined to broaden the purposes to achieve several objectives. Frequently, the broadening is well intentioned, aiming to increase the apparent efficiency of the process and to increase support for its implementation. Such accommodations, however, may undermine the ultimate success of evaluations and should occur only after careful examination of the compatibility of underlying assumptions and ultimate expectations.

2. Institutions should develop a way to regularly and systematically assess program quality and to suggest ways for programs to improve. Although this effort may be linked to planning and budgeting processes, it should be a separate activity.

A good illustration of inherent conflict can be found in reviews that seek both program improvement and resource reallocation.

Writers generally agree that information on program quality and on strategies to improve them should be included in planning and budgeting processes (Craven 1980b; Hartmark 1982; Volkwein 1984). The assessments required to produce such information, however, are too important (and too time consuming) to be treated as incidental activities. Annual budgeting and, to a certain extent, planning tend to overwhelm other considerations because of the immediacy of the decisions being made. Information about program quality will be sought in varying degrees in making such decisions, but it is unrealistic to assume that those responsible for planning and budgeting have the time and energy required for thorough assessments of quality. An institution's interests are best served if the assessment of quality and the development of budget plans are undertaken separately.

Processes

3. It is unlikely that institutions will be able to design an evaluation system that strictly conforms with any of the evaluation models suggested to date. The value of the models is not in the wholesale adoption of a particular one but in the selective use of features from several.

This review of currently used program review models suggests that most are, to a large extent, based on objectives. Reviewers are logically drawn to an evaluation system that looks at congruence between original plans and subsequent performance. This appeal partly explains why the responsive (or goal-free) model has not been popular. It can be hard to attract support for an evaluation process in which program goals do not provide the centerpiece for the evaluation. What the responsive model can contribute to an evaluation system, however, is a sensitivity to unintended results and to the need to consider the perspectives of all constituencies. Thus, a feature of the decision-oriented model relevant for most institutions is the centrality of questions that need to be answered as a result of the evaluation and of those who are in a position to use the results. Finally, the connoisseurship model adds the peer perspective, a critical element in making judgments about disciplinary matters. No single model is adequate: The use of features from several different models enriches evaluations and is more likely to yield useful results.

4. Program review processes should be flexible enough to accommodate change once it appears necessary and should encourage interaction between those conducting the evaluation and those being evaluated.

A review process must be flexible. It is impossible to design a review process that anticipates all the questions that need to be addressed and all the constituencies that need to be consulted. It is useful to have a standard evaluative procedure, but standard evaluations should probably not exist. Early attention will need to be given to how a standard procedure should be altered to make it relevant in a particular situation. These kinds of adjustments require conversations early in the review process with those who have an interest in the evaluation. Such communication will need to occur throughout the evaluation to ensure that data being collected relate to original and emerging questions and to test the validity of conclusions and recommendations. This emphasis on flexibility and frequent communication has been emphasized repeatedly in the literature (Barak 1982; Brown and Braskamp 1980).

5. In designing an evaluation process, an institution should review all programs on a cyclical basis rather than selected programs on an ad hoc basis.

Most institutions reviewed in this study have established a review process in which all programs are evaluated cyclically. This arrangement has the advantage of making program review a routine activity, one in which the advent of a review does not raise anxieties prematurely. Those institutions that conduct ad hoc reviews in response to problems are likely to find themselves faced with the need to justify the review continuously and to deal with apprehensions about the review at every stage of the process. It will not take long for program participants to learn that those programs designated for review have problems—hardly a healthy context in which to carry out a review.

6. Very few evaluative questions can be answered with any degree of certainty on the basis of a single indicator. Most questions have multiple dimensions, and multiple indicators will be required for their assessment.

The indicators to use in making evaluative judgments are never straightforward. Opinions range widely about how this task should be done, what measures should be used, and what the results mean. Similar debates have occurred

with respect to assessing a program's demand, centrality, uniqueness, efficiency, and effectiveness. Each of these concepts includes a number of indicators that one might suggest, but it is unlikely that any one will suffice. The consensus in the literature is that most evaluative questions are best addressed by collecting data from multiple sources (Brown and Braskamp 1980; Clark, Hartnett, and Baird 1976a, 1976b; DiBiaso et al. 1981; Lawrence and Green 1980). This strategy recognizes the difficulty of making evaluative judgments and suggests that they are more likely to be accurate if different dimensions are measured and different perspectives solicited.

7. *Provided quality is assessed in a multidimensional way, the number and variety of quality indicators identified to date provide a basis for making reasonable judgments about the strengths and limitations of programs.*

The several strategies for assessing quality discussed in this monograph provide some insight into program quality. Considerable attention has been given to assessing faculty research, somewhat less to instructional quality. Attempts to assess instructional quality often focus on resources (success of graduates, for example) and pay little attention to program impact. This deficiency should be corrected through attention to "value-added" learning (Astin 1980). Unfortunately, most program reviews include few measures of program impact.

A great number of quantitative and qualitative indicators have been suggested for use in assessing the quality of a program (Clark, Hartnett, and Baird 1976b; Conrad and Blackburn *In press* a; Webster 1981). The specific indicators to be used and the weight to be assigned to each need to vary by institution. If quality is to be adequately assessed, however, it is imperative that institutions use diverse indicators (both quantitative and qualitative) and indicators not only of program resources and outcomes but also of value-added student learning.

8. *The use of outside reviewers need not be an integral part of every program review.*

The use of outside reviewers has great support in higher education, and their use is justified on the basis of the disciplinary perspective and wisdom added to the review. Although outside reviewers undoubtedly provide valuable insight into some matters, it also seems reasonable to assume that disciplinary questions may not always be paramount. Such issues as quality of instruction, effective leadership, student demand, centrality, and efficiency do not automatically require the perspective of outside reviewers. Furthermore, such reviews are expensive, both in terms of dollars and in terms of time. Outside reviewers should be used selectively in response to specific questions that such a perspective would help resolve.

Results

9. Institutions need to be concerned about the link between program review processes and other decision-making processes. This link will not occur automatically; it must be incorporated into the design of the review process and must be nurtured continuously.

Most evaluation processes are isolated from decision making. This problem is particularly acute at institutions where program review is conducted in one part of the institution and planning and budgeting in another. A few institutions (Ohio State University, for example) have devised procedures to ensure that the results of reviews are introduced into planning and budgeting. More typically, however, the link between evaluation and planning and budgeting does not exist. Evaluations should be linked more systematically to planning and budgeting (Arns and Poland 1980; Clifford and Sherman 1983; Craven 1980b; Hartmark 1982; Patton 1978; Stufflebeam et al. 1971).

10. Program review activities should be linked to but not drive decision-making processes.

This proposal is related to the previous one, and it serves to attenuate expectations to a reasonable level. It is important for the results of program review to be linked to decision making, but it is unreasonable to expect this link to result in a one-to-one relationship between evaluative conclusions and recommendations and subsequent actions. Just as evaluations rely on multiple indicators, decisions in other parts of the institution are improved if multiple perspectives are solicited. Those responsible for program reviews should ensure that the results constitute one source of information that is routinely consulted. Sometimes the evaluative advice should be followed; sometimes it should be ignored.

One assumption implicit in program review is that such

reviews are likely to make a positive contribution. The fact is that research on this matter is almost nonexistent. A few institutional case studies have examined whether results have been used, but the larger issue—the question of impact—has not been examined systematically. On the one hand, the continued existence and growth of program review processes suggest that such efforts are supported and that the results can be beneficial. On the other hand, numerous critics believe that such reviews do not make much difference and, in fact, may actually make things worse. Clearly, researchers and practitioners alike need to give increased attention to the assessment of the consequences of program review.

REFERENCES

The ERIC Clearinghouse on Higher Education abstracts
and indexes the current literature on higher education for
the National Institute of Education's monthly bibliographic
journal, *Resources in Education*. Most of these publications are available through the ERIC Document Reproduction Service (EDRS). For publications cited in this bibliog-
raphy that are available from EDRS, ordering number and
price are included. Readers who wish to order a publication should write to the ERIC Document Reproduction
Service, 3900 Wheeler Avenue, Alexandria, Virginia
22304. When ordering, please specify the document number. Documents are available as noted in microfiche (MF)
and paper copy (PC). Because prices are subject to change,
it is advisable to check the latest issue of *Resources in
Education* for current cost based on the number of pages in
the publication.

Alkin, Marvin C. 1972. "Evaluation Theory and Development."
In *Evaluating Action Programs: Readings in Social Action and
Education,* edited by Carol H. Weiss. Boston: Allyn & Bacon.
——. 1980. "Naturalistic Study of Evaluation Utilization." In
Utilization of Evaluative Information, edited by Larry A. Braskamp and Robert D. Brown. New Directions for Program Evaluation No. 5. San Francisco: Jossey-Bass.

Alkin, Marvin C., and Fitz-Gibbon, Carol T. Spring 1975. "Methods and Theories of Evaluating Programs." *Journal of
Research and Development in Education* 8: 2–15.

Anderson, Scarvia B., and Ball, Samuel. 1978. *The Profession
and Practice of Program Evaluation.* San Francisco: Jossey-
Bass.

Arns, Robert G., and Poland, William. May/June 1980. "Changing the University through Program Review." *Journal of
Higher Education* 51: 268–84.

Astin, Alexander W. 1980. "When Does a College Deserve to Be
Called 'High Quality'?" In *Improving Teaching and Institutional Quality.* Current Issues in Higher Education No. 1.
Washington, D.C.: American Association for Higher Education. ED 194 004. 63 pp. MF–$.97; PC not available EDRS.

Astin, Alexander W., and Solmon, Lewis C. October 1981. "Are
Reputational Ratings Needed to Measure Quality?" *Change* 13:
14–19.

Barak, Robert J. 1977. "Program Review by Statewide Higher
Education Agencies." In *Increasing the Public Accountability
of Higher Education,* edited by John K. Folger. New Directions for Institutional Research No. 16. San Francisco: Jossey-
Bass.

———. 1980. "Study of Program Review." In *Postsecondary Education Program Review*, edited by Barbara Krauth. Boulder, Colo.: Western Interstate Commission on Higher Education.

———. 1981. "Program Evaluation as a Tool for Retrenchment." In *Challenges of Retrenchment*, edited by James R. Mingle et al. San Francisco: Jossey-Bass.

———. 1982. *Program Review in Higher Education: Within and Without*. Boulder, Colo.: National Center for Higher Education Management Systems. ED 246 829. 137 pp. MF–$.97; PC–$12.96.

———. March 1984. "State-Level Academic Program Review and Approval: 1984 Update." A paper prepared for the In-service Education Project of the State Higher Education Executive Officers, Denver, Colorado.

Barak, Robert J., and Berdahl, Robert O. 1978. *State-Level Academic Program Review in Higher Education*. Denver: Education Commission of the States. ED 158 638. 141 pp. MF–$.97; PC–$12.96.

Barak, Robert J., and Engdahl, Lilla. 1980. "Study of Academic Program Review." In *Postsecondary Education Program Review*, edited by Barbara Krauth. Boulder, Colo.: Western Interstate Commission on Higher Education.

Barker, Roger G. 1968. *Ecological Psychology*. Stanford, Calif.: Stanford University Press.

Berdahl, Robert. 1971. *Statewide Coordination of Higher Education*. Washington, D.C.: American Council on Education.

———. 1977. "Legislative Program Evaluation." In *Increasing the Public Accountability of Higher Education*, edited by John K. Folger. New Directions for Institutional Research No. 16. San Francisco: Jossey-Bass.

Berve, Nancy W. 1975. *Survey of the Structure of State Coordinating or Governing Boards and Public Institutional and Multi-campus Governing Boards of Postsecondary Education*. Denver: Education Commission of the States. ED 105 805. 57 pp. MF–$.97; PC–$7.14.

Blackburn, Robert T., and Lingenfelter, Paul E. 1973. *Assessing Quality in Academic Programs: Criteria and Correlates of Excellence*. Ann Arbor: University of Michigan, Center for the Study of Higher Education.

Bogue, E. Grady. 1980. "State Agency Approaches to Academic Program Evaluation." In *Academic Program Evaluation*, edited by Eugene C. Craven. New Directions for Institutional Research No. 27. San Francisco: Jossey-Bass.

Braskamp, Larry A. 1982. "Evaluation Systems Are More Than Information Systems." In *Designing Academic Program*

Reviews, edited by Richard F. Wilson. New Directions for Higher Education No. 37. San Francisco: Jossey-Bass.

Braskamp, Larry A., and Brown, Robert D. 1980. "Editors' Notes." In *Utilization of Evaluative Information,* edited by Larry A. Braskamp and Robert D. Brown. New Directions for Program Evaluation No. 5. San Francisco: Jossey-Bass.

British Columbia Institute of Technology. July 1979. *Program Assessment Manual.* Burnaby, B. C.: British Columbia Institute of Technology.

Brown, Robert D., and Braskamp, Larry A. 1980. "Summary: Common Themes and a Checklist." In *Utilization of Evaluative Information,* edited by Larry A. Braskamp and Robert D. Brown. New Directions for Program Evaluation No. 5. San Francisco: Jossey-Bass.

Burke, Colin B. 1982. *American Collegiate Populations: A Test of the Traditional View.* New York: Columbia University Press.

Cartter, Allen M. 1966. *An Assessment of Quality in Graduate Education.* Washington, D.C.: American Council on Education.

Clark, Mary Jo. 1977. "Program Review Practices of University Departments." Princeton, N.J.: Educational Testing Service. ED 155 959. 13 pp. MF–$.97; PC–$3.54.

Clark, Mary Jo; Hartnett, Rodney T.; and Baird, Leonard L. 1976a. *Assessing Dimensions of Quality in Doctoral Education: A Technical Report of a National Study of Three Fields.* Princeton, N.J.: Educational Testing Service. ED 173 144. 427 pp. MF–$.97; PC–$36.22.

————. 1976b. *The Assessment of Quality in Graduate Education: Summary of a Multidimensional Approach.* Princeton, N.J.: Educational Testing Service.

Clifford, David L., and Sherman, Paul. 1983. "Internal Evaluation: Integrating Program Evaluation and Management." In *Developing Effective Internal Evaluation,* edited by Arnold J. Love. New Directions for Program Evaluation No. 20. San Francisco: Jossey-Bass.

Clugston, Richard M., Jr. March 1984. "Academic Programs in an Era of Decline: The Survival of the Fittest?" Paper presented at the annual meeting of the Association for the Study of Higher Education, Chicago.

Cochran, Thomas R., and Hengstler, Dennis D. 1984. "Political Processes in an Academic Audit: Linking Evaluative Information to Programmatic Decisions." *Research in Higher Education* 20: 181–92.

Conrad, Clifton F. 1978. *The Undergraduate Curriculum: A Guide to Innovation and Reform.* Boulder, Colo.: Westview.

————. Summer 1982. "Grounded Theory: An Alternative Approach to Research in Higher Education." *The Review of Higher Education* 5: 239–49.

————. 1983. "Enhancing Institutional and Program Quality." In *Survival in the 1980s: Quality, Mission, and Financing Options,* edited by Robert A. Wilson. Tucson: Center for the Study of Higher Education. ED 236 994. 296 pp. MF–$.97; PC not available EDRS.

Conrad, Clifton F., and Blackburn, Robert T. 1985. "Research on Program Quality: A Review and Critique of the Literature." In *Higher Education: Handbook of Theory and Research,* vol. 1, edited by John C. Smart. New York: Agathon Press.

————. In press *a.* "Correlates of Departmental Quality in Regional Colleges and Universities." *American Educational Research Journal.*

————. In press *b.* "Current Views of Departmental Quality: An Empirical Examination." *Review of Higher Education.*

Conrad, Clifton F., and Wyer, Jean C. 1980. *Liberal Education in Transition.* AAHE-ERIC Higher Education Research Report No. 3. Washington, D.C.: American Association for Higher Education. ED 188 539. 73 pp. MF–$.97; PC–$7.14.

Cranton, P. A., and Legge, L. H. September/October 1978. "Program Evaluation in Higher Education." *Journal of Higher Education* 49: 464–71.

Craven, Eugene C. 1980a. "A Concluding Perspective." In *Academic Program Evaluation,* edited by Eugene C. Craven. New Directions for Institutional Research No. 27. San Francisco: Jossey-Bass.

————. 1980b. "Evaluating Program Performance." In *Improving Academic Management,* edited by Paul Jedamus, Marvin Peterson, et al. San Francisco: Jossey-Bass.

Cronbach, Lee J. April 1977. "Remarks to the New Society." *Evaluation Research Society Newsletter* 1: 1–3.

Denzin, Norman K. 1978. *The Research Act.* New York: McGraw-Hill.

DiBiaso, Daniel A., and Ecker, George. March 1982. "Academic Program Review as a Loosely Coupled System." Paper presented at the annual meeting of the American Educational Research Association, New York.

DiBiaso, Daniel A., et al. May 1981. "Assessing Quality in Graduate Programs: An Internal Quality Indicator." Paper presented at the annual forum of the Association for Institutional Research, Minneapolis. ED 205 084. 29 pp. MF–$.97; PC–$5.34.

Dolan, W. Patrick. 1976. *The Ranking Game.* Lincoln, Neb.: University of Nebraska Printing and Duplicating Service.

Dougherty, Edward A. April 1979. "What Is the Most Effective Way to Handle Program Discontinuance?" Paper presented at the annual meeting of the American Association for Higher Education, Chicago. ED 181 789. 42 pp. MF–$.97; PC–$5.34.

———. 1981. "Evaluating and Discontinuing Programs." In *Challenges of Retrenchment,* edited by James R. Mingle, et al. San Francisco: Jossey-Bass.

Dressel, Paul L. 1976. *Handbook of Academic Evaluation.* San Francisco: Jossey-Bass.

———. 1982. "Values (Virtues and Vices) in Decision Making." In *Designing Academic Program Reviews,* edited by Richard F. Wilson. New Directions for Higher Education No. 37. San Francisco: Jossey-Bass.

Eisner, Elliot W. December 1975. "The Perceptive Eye: Toward the Reformation of Educational Evaluation." Stanford, Calif.: Stanford Evaluation Consortium.

Feasley, Charles E. 1980. *Program Evaluation.* AAHE-ERIC Higher Education Research Report No. 2. Washington, D.C.: American Association for Higher Education. ED 187 269. 68 pp. MF–$.97; PC–$7.14.

Fincher, Cameron; Furniss, W. Todd; Mingle, James R.; and Spence, David S. 1978. *The Closing System of Academic Employment.* Atlanta: Southern Regional Education Board. ED 160 032. 82 pp. MF–$.97; PC–$9.36.

Floyd, Carol E. March 1983. "Balancing State and Institutional Perspectives in the Implementation of Effective State-Level Academic Program Review." A paper presented at the annual meeting of the Association for the Study of Higher Education, Washington, D.C. ED 232 551. 21 pp. MF–$.97; PC–$3.54.

Folger, John K. 1977. "Editor's Notes." In *Increasing the Public Accountability of Higher Education,* edited by John K. Folger. New Directions for Institutional Research No. 16. San Francisco: Jossey-Bass.

Gardner, Don E. September/October 1977. "Five Evaluation Frameworks: Implications for Decision Making in Higher Education." *Journal of Higher Education* 8: 571–93.

Garfinkel, Harold. 1967. *Studies in Ethnomethodology.* Englewood Cliffs, N.J.: Prentice-Hall.

Gentile, Arthur C. February 1980. "A Model for Internal Review." *Communication* 12: 4–7.

George, Melvin D. 1982. "Assessing Program Quality." In *Designing Academic Program Reviews,* edited by Richard F. Wilson. New Directions for Higher Education No. 37. San Francisco: Jossey-Bass.

Glaser, Barney G., and Strauss, Anselm. 1967. *The Discovery of Grounded Theory: Strategies for Qualitative Research.* Chicago: Aldine.

Glenny, Lyman A.; Shea, John R.; Ruyle, Janet H.; and Freschi, Kathryn H. 1976. *Presidents Confront Reality: From Edifice Complex to University without Walls.* A report for the Carnegie Council on Policy Studies in Higher Education. San Francisco: Jossey-Bass.

Graduate Council. March 1983. "Guidelines for Graduate Program Review." Photocopied. Lawrence, Kansas: University of Kansas.

Green, Kenneth C. January/February 1981. "Program Review and the State Responsibility for Higher Education." *Journal of Higher Education* 52: 67–80.

Groves, Roderick T. Fall 1979. "Program Review in a Multilevel State Governance System: The Case of Illinois." *Planning for Higher Education* 8: 1–9.

Guba, Egon G., and Lincoln, Yvonna S. 1981. *Effective Evaluation: Improving the Usefulness of Evaluation Results through Responsive and Naturalistic Approaches.* San Francisco: Jossey-Bass.

Harcleroad, Fred F. 1980. "The Context of Academic Program Evaluation." In *Academic Program Evaluation,* edited by Eugene C. Craven. New Directions for Institutional Research No. 27. San Francisco: Jossey-Bass.

Hartmark, Leif S. December 1982. "A Planning, Budgeting, and Evaluation System: Lessons from Experience." A paper presented at the Third Annual Conference on Higher Education Finance, University of Arizona.

Hill, Joan A.; Lutterbie, Patricia H.; and Stafford, Joseph H. April 1979. "Systemwide Academic Program Review: The Florida Plan." A paper presented at the annual conference of the American Association for Higher Education, Washington, D.C. ED 181 792. 11 pp. MF–$.97; PC–$3.54.

Hines, Edward R. October/November 1980. "Assessing Quality and Excellence in Higher Education: The Mutually Complementary Roles of Campus and State." Paper presented at the annual meeting of the Northeast Association for Institutional Research.

House, Ernest R. March 1978. "Assumptions Underlying Evaluation Models." *Educational Researcher* 7: 4–12.

———. 1982. "Alternative Evaluation Strategies in Higher Education." In *Designing Academic Program Reviews,* edited by Richard F. Wilson. New Directions for Higher Education No. 37. San Francisco: Jossey-Bass.

House, Ernest, and Allarie, Sandra. February 1982. "Goal-Free Evaluation." *State Evaluation Network* 2: 9–12.

Jones, L. V.; Lindzey, G.; and Coggeshall, P. E., eds. 1982. *An*

Assessment of Research-Doctorate Programs in the United States. 5 vol. Washington, D.C.: National Academy Press.

Kansas Board of Regents. 1984. "Program Review in the Regents System." Photocopied. Topeka, Kansas: Board of Regents.

Kuh, George D. 1981. *Indices of Quality in the Undergraduate Experience.* AAHE-ERIC Higher Education Research Report No. 4. Washington, D.C.: American Association for Higher Education. ED 213 340. 50 pp. MF–$.97; PC–$5.34.

Lawrence, Judith K., and Green, Kenneth C. 1980. *A Question of Quality: The Higher Education Ratings Game.* AAHE-ERIC Higher Education Research Report No. 5. Washington, D.C.: American Association for Higher Education. ED 192 667. 76 pp. MF–$.97; PC–$9.36.

Lee, Eugene C., and Bowen, Frank M. 1971. *The Multicampus University: A Study of Academic Governance.* New York: McGraw-Hill.

———. 1975. *Managing Multicampus Systems.* San Francisco: Jossey-Bass.

Melchiori, Gerlinda S. 1980. "Patterns of Program Discontinuance: A Comparative Analysis of State Agency Procedures for Initiating and Implementing the Discontinuance of Academic Programs." Ph.D. dissertation, University of Michigan.

———. 1982. *Planning for Program Discontinuance: From Default to Design.* AAHE-ERIC Higher Education Research Report No. 5. Washington, D.C.: American Association for Higher Education. ED 224 451. 58 pp. MF–$.97; PC–$7.14.

Millard, Richard M. 1976. *State Boards of Higher Education.* AAHE-ERIC Higher Education Research Report No. 4. Washington, D.C.: American Association for Higher Education. ED 129 196. 77 pp. MF–$.97; PC–$9.36.

Mims, R. Sue. May 1978. "Program Review and Evaluation: Designing and Implementing the Review Process." Paper presented at the annual meeting of the Association for Institutional Research, Houston. ED 192 629. 32 pp. MF–$.97; PC–$5.34.

Mines, R. A.; Gressard, Charles F.; and Daniels, Harry. May 1982. "Evaluation in the Student Services: A Metamodel." *Journal of College Student Personnel* 23: 195–201.

Mingle, James R. 1978. "Influencing Academic Outcomes: The Power and Impact of Statewide Program Review." In *The Closing System of Academic Employment,* edited by Cameron Fincher, W. Todd Furniss, James R. Mingle, and David S. Spence. Atlanta: Southern Regional Education Board. ED 160 032. 82 pp. MF–$.97; PC–$9.36.

———. 1981. "Choices Facing Higher Education in the 1980s." In *Challenges of Retrenchment,* edited by James R. Mingle and Associates. San Francisco: Jossey-Bass.

Mingle, James R., and Norris, Donald M. 1981. "Institutional Strategies for Responding to Decline." In *Challenges of Retrenchment,* edited by James R. Mingle and Associates. San Francisco: Jossey-Bass.

Mingle, James R., and Associates. 1981. *Challenges of Retrenchment.* San Francisco: Jossey-Bass.

Mintzberg, H. 1973. *The Nature of Managerial Work.* New York: Harper & Row.

Morrison, Samuel E. 1935. *The Founding of Harvard College.* Cambridge: Harvard University Press.

Munitz, Barry A., and Wright, Douglas J. 1980. "Institutional Approaches to Academic Program Evaluation." In *Academic Program Evaluation,* edited by Eugene C. Craven. New Directions for Institutional Research No. 27. San Francisco: Jossey-Bass.

Office of Academic Affairs. 1982. *Council on Program Evaluation: Second Cycle Evaluation Procedure.* Champaign, Ill.: The University of Illinois at Urbana/Champaign.

Office of Academic Affairs/Graduate School. 1978. *Guide for Program Reviewers.* Columbus: Ohio State University.

Office of the Associate Vice President for Academic Affairs/Dean of Graduate Studies. n.d. "Section 6—Program Review." Photocopied. Long Beach, Calif.: California State University–Long Beach.

Office of the Provost. January 1984. *University of Tennessee, Knoxville Academic Program Reviews.* Knoxville: University of Tennessee.

Olscamp, Paul J. September/October 1978. "Can Program Quality Be Quantified?" *Journal of Higher Education* 49: 504–11.

O'Reilly, Charles. 1981. "Evaluation Information and Decision Making in Organizations: Some Constraints on the Utilization of Evaluation Research." In *Evaluation in School Districts: Organizational Perspectives,* edited by Adrianne Bank and Richard C. Williams. Los Angeles: UCLA, Center for the Study of Evaluation.

Orlans, Harold. 1975. *Private Accreditation and Public Eligibility.* Lexington, Mass.: D. C. Heath.

Pace, C. R. February 1972. "Thoughts on Evaluation in Higher Education." Presentation for the American College Testing Program and the College of Education, University of Iowa, Iowa City. ED 066 132. 19 pp. MF–$.97; PC–$3.54.

Parlett, Malcolm, and Deardon, Garry, eds. 1977. *Introduction to Illuminative Evaluation.* Berkeley, Calif.: Pacific Soundings Press.

Patton, Michael Quinn. 1978. *Utilization-Focused Evaluation.* Beverly Hills, Calif.: Sage Publications.

————. 1980. *Qualitative Evaluation Methods*. Beverly Hills, Calif.: Sage Publications.

————. 1981. *Creative Evaluation*. Beverly Hills, Calif.: Sage Publications.

————. 1982. "Qualitative Methods and Approaches: What Are They?" In *Qualitative Methods for Institutional Research*, edited by Eileen Kuhns and S. V. Martorana. New Directions for Institutional Research No. 34. San Francisco: Jossey-Bass.

————. April 1985. "Six Honest Serving Men for Evaluation." Paper presented at the annual meeting of the American Education Research Association, Chicago.

Pelto, P. H., and Pelto, G. H. 1978. *Anthropological Research: The Structure of Inquiry*. Cambridge, England: Cambridge University Press.

Petrie, Hugh G. 1982. "Program Evaluation As an Adaptive System." In *Designing Academic Program Reviews*, edited by Richard F. Wilson. New Directions for Higher Education No. 37. San Francisco: Jossey-Bass.

Poland, William. May 1981. "Program Review at the Ohio State University." Paper presented at the annual forum of the Association for Institutional Research, Minneapolis.

Popham, W. James. 1975. *Educational Evaluation*. Englewood Cliffs, N.J.: Prentice-Hall.

Poulton, Nick L. May 1978. "Program Review and Evaluation: Integrating Results into Decision Making." Paper presented at the annual meeting of the Association for Institutional Research, Houston. ED 192 629. 32 pp. MF–$.97; PC–$5.34.

Provus, Malcolm M. 1971. *Discrepancy Evaluation*. Berkeley, Calif.: McCutchan.

Rabineau, Louis. 1983. *Postsecondary Program Review*. Issuegram 40. Denver: Education Commission of the States.

Rogers, Terry H., and Gamson, Zelda F. Summer 1982. "Evaluation as a Developmental Process: The Case of Liberal Education." *Review of Higher Education* 5: 225–38.

Roose, Kenneth D., and Anderson, Charles J. 1970. *A Rating of Graduate Programs*. Washington, D.C.: American Council on Education. ED 046 345. 14 pp. MF–$.97; PC–$3.54.

Rossi, Peter H., and Freeman, Howard A. 1982. *Evaluation: A Systematic Approach*. Beverly Hills, Calif.: Sage Publications.

Russo, J. Robert; Brown, David G.; and Rothweiler, James G. Spring 1977. "A Model for Internal Program Review." *College and University* 52: 288–98.

Scott, Robert A. Winter 1980. "Quality: Program Review's Missing Link." *College Board Review* 118: 18–21 + .

Scriven, Michael. 1967. "The Methodology of the Evaluation."

In *Perspectives of Curriculum Evaluation,* edited by Ralph Winfred Tyler, Robert M. Gagne, and Michael Scriven. AERA Monograph Series on Curriculum Evaluation. Chicago: Rand McNally.

——. December 1972. "Prose and Cons about Goal-Free Evaluation." *Evaluation Comment* 3: 1–4.

——. 1973. "Goal-Free Evaluation." In *School Evaluation: The Politics and Process,* edited by Ernest R. House. Berkeley, Calif.: McCutchan.

Seagren, Alan T., and Bean, John P. May 1981. "Evaluating Academic Programs: Alternative Purposes, Procedures, and Results." Paper presented at the annual meeting of the Association for Institutional Research, Minneapolis.

Seeley, John. 1981. "Program Review and Evaluation." In *Evaluation of Management and Planning Systems,* edited by Nick L. Poulton. New Directions for Institutional Research No. 31. San Francisco: Jossey-Bass.

Shirley, Robert C., and Volkwein, J. Fredericks. September/October 1978. "Establishing Academic Program Priorities." *Journal of Higher Education* 49: 472–88.

Skubal, Jacqueline M. 1979. "State-Level Review of Existing Academic Programs: Have Resources Been Saved?" *Research in Higher Education* 2: 223–32.

Smith, Donald K. 1980. "Multicampus System Approaches to Academic Program Evaluation." In *Academic Program Evaluation,* cited by Eugene C. Craven. New Directions for Institutional Research No. 27. San Francisco: Jossey-Bass.

Smith, Glenn P. January 1981. "Districtwide Program Review—1980–81." San Mateo County Community College District. ED 217 952. 30 pp. MF–$.97; PC–$5.34.

Smith, S. 1979. "Program Review: How Much Can We Expect?" Unpublished report. Berkeley, Calif.: University of California–Berkeley.

Smock, H. Richard. 1982. "Planning for an Evaluation Network and Institutionalization." In *Designing Academic Program Reviews,* edited by Richard F. Wilson. New Directions for Higher Education No. 37. San Francisco: Jossey-Bass.

Solmon, Lewis C. 1981. "A Multidimensional Approach to Quality." In *Quality—Higher Education's Principal Challenge,* edited by Thomas M. Stauffer. Washington, D.C.: American Council on Education.

Southern Regional Education Board. 1977. *Issues in Higher Education* No. 11. Atlanta: Southern Regional Education Board.

Stake, Robert E. April 1967. "The Countenance of Educational Evaluation." *Teachers College Record* 68: 523–40.

——, ed. 1975. *Evaluating the Arts in Education: A Responsive*

Approach. Columbus, Ohio: Merrill.

————. February 1978. "The Case Study Method in Social Inquiry." *Educational Researcher* 7: 5–8.

Stark, Joan S., and Lowther, Malcolm. 1980. "Measuring Higher Education Quality." In *Research in Higher Education* 13: 283–87.

Stefkovich, J., and Bolmin, L. 1984. "Retrenchment at the University of Missouri." Photocopied. Paper prepared for the Harvard University Institute for Educational Management.

Stufflebeam, Daniel L., et al. 1971. *Educational Evaluation and Decision Making*. Itasca, Ill.: Peacock.

Thelin, John. Winter 1984. "Methods to Their Madness: The Case for Qualitative Research." *Review of Higher Education* 7: 179–86.

Trenton State College. November 1984. "Procedures for Program Review." Photocopied. Hillcrest Lakes, Conn.: Trenton State College.

Triton College. 1979. *Program Review*. River Grove, Ill.: Triton College.

Tyler, Ralph W. 1949. *Basic Principles of Curriculum and Instruction: Syllabus for Education 360*. Chicago: University of Chicago Press.

University Council on Graduate Study. 1980. *Guidelines for Conducting Evaluations of Graduate Programs*. Pittsburgh: University of Pittsburgh.

University of Colorado–Boulder. n.d. "Procedures for Program Review at UCB." Photocopied. Boulder: University of Colorado–Boulder.

University of North Dakota. 1983. "UND Program Evaluation Process." Photocopied. Grand Forks, N.D.: University of North Dakota.

Utah Technical College at Salt Lake. n.d. "Self-Evaluation Report." Photocopied. Salt Lake City: Utah Technical College at Salt Lake.

Volkwein, J. Fredericks. May/June 1984. "Responding to Financial Retrenchment." *Journal of Higher Education* 55: 389–401.

Wallhaus, Robert A. 1982. "Process Issues in State-Level Program Reviews." In *Designing Academic Program Reviews*, edited by Richard F. Wilson. New Directions for Higher Education No. 37. San Francisco: Jossey-Bass.

Webster, David S. October 1981. "Advantages and Disadvantages of Methods of Assessing Quality." *Change* 13: 20–24.

Weiss, Carol H. 1972. *Evaluation Research: Methods for Assessing Program Effectiveness*. Englewood Cliffs, N.J.: Prentice-Hall.

Wilson, Richard F. November/December 1980. "Institutional Participation and Reciprocity in State-Level Program Reviews." *Journal of Higher Education* 6: 601–15.

————. 1982a. "Concluding Statement and Additional Readings." In *Designing Academic Program Reviews,* edited by Richard F. Wilson. New Directions for Higher Education No. 37. San Francisco: Jossey-Bass.

————, ed. 1982b. *Designing Academic Program Reviews.* New Directions for Higher Education No. 37. San Francisco: Jossey-Bass.

————. Winter 1984. "Critical Issues in Program Evaluation." *Review of Higher Education* 7: 143–57.

Wilson, Richard F., and Miller, James L., Jr. 1980. *Private College Participation in Planning and Program Review Activities of Forty-five State-Level Higher Education Agencies.* Ann Arbor: University of Michigan, Center for the Study of Higher Education.

Wood, Lynn, and Davis, Barbara Gross. 1978. *Designing and Evaluating Higher Education Curricula.* AAHE-ERIC Higher Education Research Report No. 8. Washington, D.C.: American Association for Higher Education. ED 165 669. 72 pp. MF–$.97; PC–$7.14.

Worthen, Blaine R., and Sanders, James R. 1973. *Educational Evaluation: Theory and Practice.* Worthington, Ohio: Charles A. Jones.

INDEX

ASHE-ERIC HIGHER EDUCATION REPORTS

Starting in 1983, the Association for the Study of Higher Education assumed cosponsorship of the Higher Education Reports with the ERIC Clearinghouse on Higher Education. For the previous 11 years, ERIC and the American Association for Higher Education prepared and published the reports.

Each report is the definitive analysis of a tough higher education problem, based on a thorough research of pertinent literature and institutional experiences. Report topics, identified by a national survey, are written by noted practitioners and scholars with prepublication manuscript reviews by experts.

Eight monographs (10 monographs before 1985) in the ASHE-ERIC Higher Education Report series are published each year, available individually or by subscription. Subscription to eight issues is $55 regular; $40 for members of AERA, AAHE and AIR: $35 for members of ASHE. (Add $7.50 outside the United States.)

Prices for single copies, including 4th class postage and handling, are $7.50 regular and $6.00 for members of AERA, AAHE, AIR, and ASHE ($6.50 regular and $5.00 for members for reports published before 1983). If faster 1st class postage is desired for U.S. and Canadian orders, add $.75 for each publication ordered: overseas, add $4.50. For VISA and MasterCard payments, include card number, expiration date, and signature. Orders under $25 must be prepaid. Bulk discounts are available on orders of 15 or more reports (not applicable to subscriptions). Order from the Publications Department, Association for the Study of Higher Education, One Dupont Circle, Suite 630, Washington, D.C. 20036, (202 296-2597. Write for a publication list of all the Higher Education Reports available.

1985 Higher Education Reports

1. Flexibility in Academic Staffing: Effective Policies and Practices
   Kenneth P. Mortimer, Marque Bagshaw, and Andrew T. Masland

2. Associations in Action: The Washington, D.C., Higher Education Community
   Harland G. Bloland

3. And on the Seventh Day: Faculty Consulting and Supplemental Income
   Carol M. Boyer and Darrell R. Lewis

4. Faculty Research Performance: Lessons from the Sciences and Social Sciences
   John W. Creswell

5. Academic Program Reviews: Institutional Approaches, Expectations, and Controversies
   Clifton F. Conrad and Richard F. Wilson

1984 Higher Education Reports

1. Adult Learning: State Policies and Institutional Practices
   K. Patricia Cross and Anne-Marie McCartan

2. Student Stress: Effects and Solutions
   Neal A. Whitmar, David C. Spendlove, and Claire H. Clark

---

3. Part-time Faculty: Higher Education at a Crossroads
Judith M. Gappa

4. Sex Discrimination Law in Higher Education: The Lessons of the Past Decade
J. Ralph Lindgren, Patti T. Ota, Perry A. Zirkel, and Nan Van Gieson

5. Faculty Freedoms and Institutional Accountability: Interactions and Conflicts
Steven G. Olswang and Barbara A. Lee

6. The High-Technology Connection: Academic Industrial Cooperation for Economic Growth
Lynn G. Johnson

7. Employee Educational Programs: Implications for Industry and Higher Education
Suzanne W. Morse

8. Academic Libraries: The Changing Knowledge Centers of Colleges and Universities
Barbara B. Moran

9. Futures Research and the Strategic Planning Process: Implications for Higher Education
James L. Morrison, William L. Renfro, and Wayne I. Boucher

10. Faculty Workload: Research, Theory, and Interpretation
Harold E. Yuker

1983 Higher Education Reports

1. The Path to Excellence: Quality Assurance in Higher Education
Laurence R. Marcus, Anita O. Leone, and Edward D. Goldberg

2. Faculty Recruitment, Retention, and Fair Employment: Obligations and Opportunities
John S. Waggaman

3. Meeting the Challenges: Developing Faculty Careers
Michael C. T. Brookes and Katherine L. German

4. Raising Academic Standards: A Guide to Learning Improvement
Ruth Talbott Keimig

5. Serving Learners at a Distance: A Guide to Program Practices
Charles E. Feasley

6. Competence, Admissions, and Articulation: Returning to the Basics in Higher Education
Jean L. Preer

7. Public Service in Higher Education: Practices and Priorities
Patricia H. Crosson

8. Academic Employment and Retrenchment: Judicial Review and Administrative Action
Robert M. Hendrickson and Barbara A. Lee

9. Burnout: The New Academic Disease
Winifred Albizu Meléndez and Rafael M. de Guzmán

10. Academic Workplace: New Demands, Heightened Tensions
Ann E. Austin and Zelda F. Gamson